ITALIAN
TRAVELMATE

compiled by
LEXUS
with
Annelisa Franchini

Chambers

by Richard Drew Publishing Ltd
Reprinted 1982, 1984
Second edition 1988
Reprinted 1988, 1989, 1990

This edition published 1991 by W & R Chambers Ltd,
43–45 Annandale Street, Edinburgh EH7 4AZ
Reprinted 1992

**British Library Cataloguing in
Publication Data**

A catalogue record for this book is
available from the British Library

ISBN 0-550-22002-X

Printed and bound in Great Britain by
Cox & Wyman Ltd

YOUR TRAVELMATE

gives you one single easy-to-use list of words and phrases to help you communicate in Italian.

Built into this list are:
– Travel Tips with facts and figures which provide valuable information
– Italian words you'll see on signs and notices
– typical replies to some of the things you might want to say.

There is a menu reader on pages 70–71, the Italian alphabet is given on page 127 and numbers on page 128.

Your TRAVELMATE also tells you how to pronounce Italian. Just read the pronunciations as though they were English and you will communicate – although you might not sound like a native speaker.

If no pronunciation is given then the word itself can be pronounced as though it were English. And sometimes only part of a word or phrase needs a pronunciation guide. Vowels given in italics show which part of a word to stress.

a, an un, una [oon, *oo*-nah].
   800 lire a litre ottocento lire al litro
   [ot-toh-ch*e*n-toh l*ee*-ray . . .]
abdomen l'addome [ad-d*oh*-may]
aboard a bordo
about: is the manager about? c'è il direttore?
   [cheh eel dee-rayt-*toh*-ray]
   about 15 circa quindici [ch*e*er-kah
   kw*ee*n-dee-chee]
   about 2 o'clock verso le due [. . . d*oo*-ay]
above sopra
abroad all'estero [al-l*e*s-tay-roh]
absolutely! certo! [ch*a*yr-toh]
accelerator l'acceleratore
   [la-chay-lay-ra-t*oh*-ray]
accendere i fari switch on headlights
accept accettare [a-chet-t*ah*-ray]
accident un incidente [een-chee-d*e*n-tay]
   there's been an accident è successo un
   incidente [eh soo-ch*e*s-soh . . .]
accommodation un posto da dormire
   [. . . dor-m*ee*-ray]
   we need accommodation for three c'è
   [cheh] posto da dormire per tre?
» *TRAVEL TIP: information can be obtained from
   the local tourist office, called 'Pro Loco'*
accountant un ragioniere [ra-jon-y*e*h-ray]
accurate accur*a*to
ache un dolore [doh-l*oh*-ray]
   my back aches mi fa mal la schiena [mee fah
   mal lah skee-*a*y-nah]
ACI = *Automobil Club d'Italia: like our AA or
   RAC*
acqua potabile drinking water

across attraverso
  how do we get across? come attraversiamo?
  [koh-may . . .]
adaptor una spina intermedia [spee-nah
  een-ter-may-dee-ah]
adjust aggiustare [ah-joos-tah-ray]
address l'indirizzo [een-dee-reet-tzoh]
  will you give me your address? mi dai il tuo
  indirizzo? [mee dah-ee . . .]
admission l'entrata
advance: can we book in advance? possiamo
  prenotare? [. . .–tah-ray]
advert un annuncio [an-noon-choh]
afraid: I'm afraid I don't know purtroppo non
  so
  I'm afraid so purtroppo sì [. . . see]
  I'm afraid not no, mi spiace [no mee
  spee-ah-chay]
after: after you dopo di lei [. . . dee lay]
  after 3 o'clock dopo le tre [. . . lay tray]
afternoon il pomeriggio [po-may-ree-joh]
  this afternoon questo pomeriggio
  in the afternoon nel pomeriggio
  good afternoon *(from morning till
  mid-afternoon)* buon giorno [bwon jor-noh]
  (after that) buona sera [bwo-nah say-rah]
aftershave il dopobarba
again ancora
against contro
age l'età [ay-tah]
  under age minorenne [mee-no-ren-nay]
  it takes ages ci vogliono anni [chee
  vol-yoh-noh an-nee]
ago: a week ago una settimana fa
  it wasn't long ago non tanto tempo fa
  how long ago was that? quanto tempo fa?
agree: I agree sono d'accordo
  it doesn't agree with me non mi fa bene [non
  mee fah bay-nay]

air l'aria [*ah*-ree-ah]
  by air in aereo [een ah-*eh*-ray-oh]
  by airmail per posta aerea [. . . ah-*eh*-ray-ah]
  with air-conditioning con l'aria condizionata
  [. . . kon-dee-tzee-o-n*ah*-tah]
airport l'aeroporto [ah-ay-ro-por-toh]
alarm l'allarme [–may]
  alarm clock le sveglia [sv*ay*l-yah]
alcohol l'alcol [*a*l-kol]
  is it alcoholic? è alcolico? [eh al-k*o*-lee-koh]
alive vivo [vee-voh]
  is he still alive? è ancora vivo? [eh . . .]
all tutto [t*oo*t-toh]
  all night tutta la notte [–tay]
  that's all wrong è tutto sbagliato [eh . . .
  sbal-y*ah*-toh]
  all right va bene [. . . b*ay*-nay]
  I'm all right sto bene
  that's all è tutto
  thank you – not at all grazie – prego
  [gr*ah*-tzee ay pr*ay*-goh]
allergic allergico [al-l*e*r-jee-koh]
  I'm allergic to sono allergico a
allowed permesso
  is it allowed? è permesso?
  it's not allowed è vietato [eh vee-ay-t*ah*-toh]
  allow me mi permetta [mee . . .]
almost quasi [kw*ah*-see]
alone solo
  did you come here alone? è venuto solo?
  [eh . . .]
  leave me alone mi lasci stare [mee l*ah*-shee
  st*ah*-ray]
Alps: the Alps le Alpi [lay-*a*l-pee]
already già [djah]
also anche [*a*n-kay]
alt halt
alternator l'alternatore [–t*o*h-ray]
although sebbene [seb-b*eh*-nay]

altogether in tutto [een *toot*-toh]
  what does that make altogether? quant'è in
  tutto? [kwan-*teh* . . .]
always sempre [s*e*m-pray]
a.m. di mattina [dee mat-*tee*-nah]
ambassador l'ambasciatore
  [am-ba-sha-t*oh*-ray]
ambulance un'ambulanza [am-boo-l*a*n-tzah]
  get an ambulance! chiamate un'ambulanza!
  [kee-a-m*ah*-tay . . .]
» *TRAVEL TIP: Phone 113 anywhere in Italy*
America l'America [a-m*a*y-ree-kah]
American americano
among fra
anchor l'ancora [*a*n-ko-rah]
ancient Rome Roma Antica [. . . an-*tee*-kah]
and e [ay]
angry secc*a*to
  I'm very angry about it sono molto seccato al
  riguardo [. . . ree-gw*a*r-doh]
  please don't get angry non si arrabbi [non
  see ar-r*a*b-bee]
animal un animale [a-nee-m*a*h-lay]
ankle la caviglia [ka-v*ee*l-yah]
anniversary: it's our anniversary è il nostro
  annivers*a*rio [eh . . .]
annoy: he's annoying me mi sta seccando
  [mee . . .]
  it's very annoying è molto seccante
  [eh m*o*l-toh sayk-k*a*n-tay]
anorak la giacca a vento [j*a*k-kah . . .]
another: can we have another room?
  potremo avere un'altra camera?
  [. . . a-v*a*y-ray . . .]
  another beer, please un'altra birra, per
  favore [. . . fa-v*oh*-ray]
answer *(noun)* una risposta
  what was his answer? qual'è stata la sua
  risposta?

there was no answer nessuno ha risposto
[. . .ah. . .]
antifreeze l'antigelo [an-tee-j*a*y-loh]
any: have you any bananas/butter? avete
delle banane/del burro? [a-v*a*y-tay d*a*yl-lay
ba-n*a*h-nay. . .]
  I haven't got any non ne ho [non nay o]
anybody qualcuno [kwal-k*oo*-noh]
  I can't see anybody non vedo nessuno
  [. . . v*a*y-doh. . .]
anything qualcosa
  anything will do va bene tutto [vah b*a*y-nay
  t*oo*t-toh]
  I don't want anything non voglio niente [non
  vol-yoh nee-*e*n-tay]
aperitif un aperitivo [–tee-voh]
aperto open
apology una scusa [sk*oo*-sah]
  please accept my apologies mi scusi
  [mee. . .]
  I want an apology desidero le sue scuse
  [day-s*ee*-day-roh lay s*oo*-ay. . .]
appendicitis l'appendicite
[ap-pen-dee-ch*ee*-tay]
appetite l'appetito [ap-pay-t*ee*-toh]
  I've lost my appetite non ho più appetito
  [. . .o pew. . .]
apple una mela
application form il modulo [m*o*-doo-loh]
appointment: can I make an appointment?
posso avere un appuntamento?
[. . . a-v*a*y-ray. . .]
apricot un'albicocca
April aprile [a-pr*ee*-lay]
aqualung l'autorespiratore
[ow-toh-res-pee-ra-t*oh*-ray]
» *TRAVEL TIP: the use of an aqualung for
underwater fishing is forbidden in Italian
waters*

archaeology l'archeologia [–jee-ah]
area area [ah-ray-ah]
arm il braccio [brah-choh]
around see **about**
arrange: will you arrange it? ci pensa lei?
  [chee-pen-sah lay]
  it's all arranged è tutto a posto [eh . . .]
arrest: he's been arrested è stato arrestato [eh
  stah-toh . . .]
arrival l'arrivo [ar-ree-voh]
arrive arrivare [ar-ree-vah-ray]
  we only arrived yesterday siamo arrivati
  solo ieri [. . . yeh-ree]
arrivi arrivals
art l'arte [ar-tay]
  art gallery una galleria d'arte
  [gal-lay-ree-ah . . .]
arthritis l'artrite [ar-tree-tay]
artificial artificiale [ar-tee-fee-chah-lay]
artist l'artista
as: as quickly as you can il più in fretta
  possibile [eel pew een frayt-tah pos-see-bee-lay]
  as much as you can il più che può [. . . kay
  pwoh]
  do as I do faccia come me [fah-chah koh-may
  may]
  as you like come le pare [koh-may lay
  pah-ray]
ascensore lift
ashore a terra
  to go ashore sbarcare [sbar-kah-ray]
  we've run ashore siamo incagliati
  [. . . een-kal-yah-tee]
ashtray un portacenere [por-ta-chay-nay-ray]
ask chiedere [kee-ay-day-ray]
  could you ask him to do it for me? può
  chiedergli di farlo per me? [pwoh kee-ay-der-lee
  dee . . . may]
  that's not what I asked for non è quello che

ho chiesto [. . . kay o kee-*es*-toh]
asleep: he's still asleep è ancora addormentato
 [eh . . .]
asparagus gli asparagi [lee as-p*ah*-ra-jee]
aspirin un'aspirina
assistant l'assistente [–tay]
 shop assistant la commessa
asthma l'asma
at: at the café al caffè [kaf-f*eh*]
 at my hotel al mio albergo
atmosphere l'atmosfera
attenti al cane beware of the dog
attenzione caution
attitude l'atteggiamento [at-tay-ja-m*en*-toh]
attractive attraente [at-tra-*en*-tay]
 I think you're very attractive ti [tee] trovo
 molto attraente
aubergine la melanzana [may-lan-tz*ah*-nah]
August agosto
aunt la zia [tz*ee*-ah]
Australia l'Australia [ows-tr*al*-yah]
Australian australiano [ows-tral-y*ah*-noh]
Austria l'Austria [*ows*-tree-ah]
Austrian austriaco [*ows*-tree-a-koh]
authorities le autorità [ow-toh-ree-t*ah*]
automatic *(car)* un'automatica
 [ow-toh-m*ah*-tee-kah]
autostrada motorway
autumn l'autunno [ow-t*oo*n-noh]
 in the autumn in autunno
avanti cross now
away: is it far away from here? è molto
 lontano da qua? [eh . . .]
 go away! va' via! [. . . *vee*-ah]
awful terribile [ter-*ree*-bee-lay]
axle l'asse [*as*-say]
baby il bamb*i*no
 we'd like a baby-sitter vorremmo una
 baby-sitter

....

back: I've got a bad back ho il mal di schiena
[o eel mal dee skee-*ay*-nah]
I'll be back soon torno subito
[. . . *soo*-bee-toh]
is he back? è tornato? [eh . . .]
can I have my money back? posso avere
indietro il denaro? [. . . a-*vay*-ray
een-dee-*eh*-troh . . .]
come back torni indietro
I go back tomorrow ritorno domani
at the back dietro [dee-*eh*-troh]
bacon la pancetta affumicata
[pan-ch*ay*t-tah . . .]
bacon and eggs pancetta e uova [. . . ay
w*o*-vah]
bad cattivo [kat-*tee*-voh]
it's not bad non c'è male [non cheh m*ah*-lay]
too bad! pazienza! [pa-tzee-*en*-tzah]
bag una borsa; *(handbag)* una borsetta
baggage i bagagli [ee ba-g*al*-yee]
bagno *bathroom*
baker's il panettiere [pa-nayt-y*eh*-ray]
balcony il balcone [bal-k*oh*-nay]
a room with a balcony una c*a*mera con
balcone
ball una palla
ball-point pen una biro [b*ee*-roh]
banana una banana
band *(music)* l'orch*e*stra
bandage una benda
could you change the bandage? può
cambiare la benda? [pwoh kam-bee-*ah*-ray . . .]
bank la banca *(river)* la sponda
» *TRAVEL TIP: banks in Italy are open from 8.30 to*
1.30; 'bank holidays' see **'public holidays'**
bar il bar
when does the bar open? quando apre il bar?
[. . . *ah*-pray . . .]
» *TRAVEL TIP: in most bars you must pay at the cash*

*desk before ordering and show your ticket
(scontrino) at the bar*
YOU MAY HEAR ...
ritiri lo scontrino alla cassa *get your ticket at the
cash desk*
barber il barbiere [bar-bee-*ay*-ray]
bargain: it's a real bargain è proprio un affare
[... af-f*ah*-ray]
barman il barista [ba-*rees*-tah]
basket il cestino [ches-*tee*-noh]
bath il bagno [b*a*n-yoh]
can I have a bath? posso fare [f*ah*-ray] il
bagno?
could you give me a bath towel? può darmi
un asciugamano da bagno? [pwoh d*a*r-mee oon
a-shoo-ga-m*ah*-noh dah ...]
bathing costume un costume da bagno
[kos-*too*-may ...]
bathroom il bagno [b*a*n-yoh]
we want a room with a private bathroom
vorremmo una camera con bagno
can I use your bathroom? posso usare
[oo-*zah*-ray] il bagno?
battery una pila [p*ee*-lah] *(car)* la batteria
[bat-tay-*ree*-ah]
be essere [*es*-say-ray]
be ... sia ...
don't be ... non sia ...
beach la spiaggia [spee-*ah*-jah]
see you on the beach ci [chee] vediamo in
spiaggia
beans i fagioli [ee fa-j*oh*-lee]
beautiful bello
a beautiful woman una bella donna
that was a beautiful meal il pranzo era molto
buono [eel pr*a*n-tzoh *eh*-rah m*o*l-toh bwo-noh]
because perché [per-k*ay*]
because of the weather a causa del tempo [ah
k*ow*-zah ...]

....

bed il letto
  single bed/double bed letto singolo/letto
  matrimoniale [. . .–ah-lay]
  you haven't changed my bed non avete
  cambiato le lenzuola [non a-*vay*-tay
  kam-bee-*ah*-toh lay layn-tzwo-lah]
  I want to go to bed voglio andare a dormire
  [*v*ol-yoh an-d*ah*-ray ah dor-m*ee*-ray]
  bed and breakfast una pensione
  [payn-see-*oh*-nay]
bee un'ape [*ah*-pay]
beef il manzo [m*a*n-tzoh]
beer la birra [b*ee*r-rah]
  two beers, please due birre, per favore
  [d*oo*-ay b*ee*r-ray payr fa-v*oh*-ray]
before: before breakfast prima di colazione
  [pr*ee*-mah dee ko-la-tzee-*oh*-nay]
  before we leave prima di partire [. . .–ray]
  I haven't been here before non c'ero mai
  stato [non ch*eh*-roh m*ah*-ee . . .]
begin: when does it begin? quando inizia?
  [kw*a*n-doh ee-n*ee*-tzee-ah]
  I'm a beginner sono un principiante
  [. . . pr*ee*n-chee-pee-*a*n-tay]
behind dietro [dee-*eh*-troh]
  the car behind me l'auto dietro [ow-toh . . .]
believe: I don't believe you non la credo
  [. . . kr*a*y-doh]
  I believe you la credo
bell *(in hotel etc)* il campanello
belong: that belongs to me mi appartiene
  [mee ap-par-tee-*ay*-nay]
  who does this belong to? a chi appartiene?
  [ah kee . . .]
below sotto
belt la cintura [cheen-*too*-rah]
bend *(in road)* una curva [k*oo*r-vah]
berries le bacche [b*a*k-kay]
berth *(on ship)* una cuccetta [koo-ch*a*yt-tah]

beside accanto a
best migliore [meel-y*oh*-ray]
 it's the best holiday I've ever had è la
 migliore vacanza che abbia fatto
 [. . . va-k*a*n-tzah kay . . .]
better meglio [m*e*l-yoh]
 haven't you got anything better? non ha
 niente di meglio? [non ah nee-*e*n-tay dee . . .]
 are you feeling better? si sente meglio? [see
 s*e*n-tay . . .]
 I'm feeling a lot better mi [mee]
 sento molto meglio
between tra
beyond oltre [*o*l-tray]
bicycle la bicicletta [bee-chee-kl*a*yt-tah]
big grande [–day]
 a big one uno grande
 that's too big è troppo grande [eh . . .]
 it's not big enough non è grande abbastanza
 [. . . ab-bas-t*a*n-tzah]
 have you got a bigger one? ne avete uno più
 grande? [nay a-v*a*y-tay *oo*-noh pew . . .]
biglietti tickets
bikini il bikini
bill il conto
 could I have the bill, please? potrei avere il
 conto? [po-tr*a*y a-v*a*y-ray . . .]
» *TRAVEL TIP: service – see* **tipping**
binario platform
binding *(skiing)* l'attacco
bird un uccello [oo-ch*e*l-loh]
birthday il compleanno [kom-play-*a*n-noh]
 it's my birthday è il mio compleanno [eh eel
 m*ee*-oh . . .]
 happy birthday buon compleanno [bwon . . .]
biscuit un biscotto
bit: just a bit solo un po'
 a bit of that cake un pezzo di quella torta
 [p*e*t-tzoh dee . . .]

that's a bit too expensive è un po' troppo caro
a big bit un bel pezzo
bite *(noun)* un morso
  I've been bitten sono stato punto
  [. . . sta*h*-toh poon-toh] *(by dog)* sono stato
  morso
bitter *(taste)* amaro
black nero [n*a*y-roh]
  he's had a blackout è svenuto
bland blando
blanket una coperta
  I'd like another blanket vorrei un'altra
  coperta [vor-ray . . .]
bleach la candeggina [kan-day-*jee*-nah]
bleed sanguinare [san-gwee-n*a*h-ray]
  he's bleeding sanguina
bless you *(after sneeze)* salute! [–tay]
blind cieco [ch*e*h-koh]
  blind spot *(driving)* zona cieca [tz*o*-nah . . .]
blister una vescica [vay-sh*ee*-kah]
blocked bloccato
blonde una bionda [bee-*o*n-dah]
blood il sangue [s*a*n-gway]
  his blood group is . . . il suo gruppo
  sanguigno è . . . [. . . gro*o*p-poh
  san-gw*ee*n-yoh . . .]
  I've got high blood pressure ho la pressione
  alta [o lah prays-y*o*h-nay . . .]
  he needs a blood transfusion ha bisogno di
  una trasfusione [ah bee-s*o*nn-yoh dee . . .–nay]
bloody mary un bloody mary
blouse una camicetta [ka-mee-ch*a*yt-tah]
blue blu
board: full board la pensione completa
  [pen-see-*o*h-nay . . .]
  half board la mezza pensione
  [m*e*t-tzah . . .]
  boarding pass la carta d'imbarco
boat una barca

boat train treno di coincidenza con la nave
[... dee ko-een-chee-den-tzah kon lah nah-vay]
body il corpo *(dead body)* un morto
boil *(verb)* bollire [–ray]
  (noun) una pustola [poos-toh-lah]
  do we have to boil the water? dobbiamo
  bollire l'acqua?
  boiled egg un uovo alla coque [wo-voh al-lah
  kok]
bone un osso
bonnet *(car)* il cofano [ko-fa-noh]
book un libro [lee-broh]
  booking office l'ufficio prenotazioni
  [oof-fee-choh pray-no-ta-tzee-oh-nee]
  can I book a ticket to .../for ... posso
  prenotare un biglietto per ...
  [... beel-yet-toh ...]
  I'd like to book a table for two vorrei
  prenotare un tavolo per due [vor-ray
  pray-no-tah-ray oon tah-vo-lo payr doo-ay]
  bookshop una libreria [–ee-ah]
boot *(shoe)* uno stivale [stee-vah-lay]
  (car) il portabagagli [por-ta-ba-gal-yee]
booze: I had too much booze ho [o] bevuto
  troppo
border il confine [kon-fee-nay]
bored: I'm bored sono annoiato
  [an-no-yah-toh]
boring noioso [no-yoh-soh]
born: I was born in 1956 sono nato nel
  millenovecentocinquantasei [... meel-lay-
  no-vay-chen-toh-cheen-kwan-ta-say]
borrow: can I borrow ...? posso avere in
  prestito ...? [... a-vay-ray een pres-tee-toh]
boss il capo
both entrambi [en-tram-bee]
  I'll take both of them li prendo entrambi
  [lee ...]
bottle una bottiglia [bot-teel-yah]

....

bottle-opener un apribottiglia
bottom: at the bottom of the hill in fondo alla
collina
bouncer il buttafuori [boot-tah-fwo-ree]
bowels l'intestino [een-tes-*tee*-noh]
bowl una scodella
box una scatola [sk*ah*-toh-lah]
boy il ragazzo [ra-g*at*-tzoh]
boyfriend: my boyfriend il mio ragazzo
[m*ee*-oh ra-g*at*-tzoh]; *(older)* il mio amico
bra il reggiseno [reh-jee-s*ay*-noh]
bracelet il braccialetto [bra-cha-*l*ayt-toh]
brake *(noun)* il freno [fr*ay*-noh]
could you check the brakes? può controllare
i freni? [pwoh kon-trol-l*ah*-ray ee . . .]
I had to brake suddenly ho dovuto frenare
all'improvviso [o do-v*oo*-toh fray-n*ah*-ray . . .
–*vee*-soh]
he didn't brake non ha [a*h*] frenato
brandy un brandy
bread il pane [p*ah*-nay]
could we have some bread and butter?
potremmo avere del pane e burro?
[. . . a-v*ay*-ray . . .]
some more bread, please ancora del pane,
per favore [. . . fa-v*oh*-ray]
break *(verb)* rompere [rom-pay-ray]
I think I've broken my arm penso d'aver
rotto il braccio [. . . br*ah*-choh]
breakable fragile [fr*ah*-jee-lay]
breakdown un guasto [gw*a*s-toh]
I've had a breakdown ho avuto un guasto
[o . . .]
nervous breakdown l'esaurimento nervoso
[ay-zow-ree-m*en*-toh . . .]
» *TRAVEL TIP: breakdown services – phone 116*
breakfast la colazione [ko-la-tzee-*oh*-nay]
breast il petto
breath il fiato [fee-*ah*-toh]

breathe respirare [res-pee-*rah*-ray]
  I can't breathe non posso respirare
bridge il ponte [*pon*-tay]
briefcase la valigetta [va-lee-*jayt*-tal.]
**brighten up: do you think it'll brighten up
  later?** pensa che si rischiarerà più tardi?
  [. . . kay see rees-kee-a-ray-*rah* pew *tar*-dee]
brilliant *(very good)* brillante [–tay]
bring portare [por-*tah*-ray]
  could you bring it to my hotel? può [pwoh]
  portarlo al mio albergo?
Britain la Gran Bretagna [. . . bray-*tan*-yah]
British inglese [een-*glay*-say]
brochure un opuscolo [o-*poos*-ko-loh]
  have you got any brochures about . . .? ha
  un opuscolo su . . .? [ah . . .]
broken rotto
  you've broken it l'ha rotto [lah . . .]
  it's broken è rotto [eh . . .]
  my room/car has been broken into mi
  hanno svaligiato la camera/l'auto [mee *a*n-noh
  sva-lee-*jah*-toh la *kah*-may-rah/*low*-toh]
brooch una spilla [*spee*l-lah]
brother: my brother mio fratello [*mee*-oh . . .]
brown marrone [mar-*roh*-nay]
  brown paper la carta da pacchi [. . . *pak*-kee]
browse: can I just browse around? posso
  curiosare? [. . . –*sah*-ray]
bruise una ammaccatura
brunette una mora
brush *(noun)* una spazzola [*spat*-tzo-lah]
  (artist's) un pennello
Brussels sprouts i cavolini di Bruxelles [. . . dee
  brook-*sel*]
bucket il secchio [*sayk*-yoh]
buffet il buffet
building un edificio [ay-dee-*fee*-choh]
bulb: the bulb's gone la lampadina è rotta
  [lam-pa-*dee*-nah eh . . .]

....

bump: he's had a bump on the head ha urtato
  la testa [ah . . .]
bumper il paraurti [pa-ra-*oor*-tee]
bunch of flowers un mazzo di fiori [m*a*t-tzoh
  dee fee-*oh*-ree]
bunk una cuccetta [koo-ch*a*yt-tah]
  bunk beds i letti a castello
buoy una boa
burglar un ladro
  they've taken all my money mi hanno rubato
  tutto il denaro [mee *a*n-noh . . .]
burnt: this meat is burnt questa carne è
  bruciata [. . . k*a*r-nay eh broo-ch*ah*-tah]
  my arms are burnt mi sono scottato le braccia
  [. . . br*ah*-chah]
  can you give me something for these burns?
  mi può dare qualcosa per queste scottature?
  [mee pwoh d*ah*-ray . . . skot-ta-*too*-ray]
bus l'autobus [*ow*-toh-boos]
  bus stop la fermata dell'autobus
  could you tell me when we get there? me lo
  può dire quando ci siamo? [may loh pwoh
  d*ee*-ray kw*a*n-doh chee see-*ah*-moh]
» *TRAVEL TIP: get tickets from machine on the bus;*
  or buy a book of tickets from news-stand or
  tobacconist; usually flat fare; in Rome and
  Milan underground tickets valid for bus travel
  up to 1 hour from issue
business: I'm here on business sono qui per
  affari [. . . kwee payr . . .]
  business trip un viaggio d'affari
  [vee-*ah*-joh . . .]
  none of your business non è affar suo
  [. . . eh . . .]
bust il busto [b*oo*s-toh]
» *TRAVEL TIP: bust measurements*

UK	32	34	36	38	40
Italy	80	87	91	97	102

busy occupato

but ma
  not this one but that one non questo ma
  quello
butcher il macellaio [ma-chel-l*ah*-yoh]
butter il burro [b*oo*r-roh]
button un bottone [bot-*toh*-nay]
buy: where can I buy . . .? dove posso
  comprare [d*oh*-vay . . . kom-pr*ah*-ray]
  I'll buy it lo compro
by: I'm here by myself sono qui [kwee] da solo
  are you by yourself? è qui da solo? [eh . . .]
  can you do it by tomorrow? può farlo per
  domani? [pwoh . . . payr . . .]
  by train/car/plane in treno/auto/aereo [een
  tr*eh*-noh/*ow*-toh/ah-*eh*-ray-oh]
  I parked by the trees ho parcheggiato vicino
  agli alberi [o par-kay-j*ah*-toh vee-ch*ee*-noh
  *a*l-yee *a*l-bay-ree]
  who's it made by? chi l'ha fatto? [kee lah . . .]
c *(on tap) hot*
cabaret il cabaret
cabbage un cavolo [k*ah*-vo-loh]
cable il cavo [k*ah*-voh]
  cable car la funivia [–*vee*-ah]
cabin *(on ship)* una cabina
caduta massi *falling rocks*
cafe un caffè [kaf-f*eh*]
» *TRAVEL TIP: Italian cafes also serve alcoholic*
  drinks, but only snacks – toasted sandwiches
  and cakes; for cafe-type food look for the sign
  'tavola calda'
cake una pasta
  a piece of cake un pezzo di torta [pet-tzoh
  dee . . .]
calculator un calcolatore [–*toh*-ray]
call: will you call the manager? mi chiama il
  direttore? [mee kee-*ah*-mah eel
  dee-rayt-*toh*-ray]
  what is this called? come si [see] chiama?

call box un telefono pubblico [tay-leh-fo-noh poob-blee-koh]

calm calmo

  calm down si calmi [see . . .]

camera la macchina fotografica [mak-kee-nah . . .]

camp: is there somewhere we can camp? dove possiamo accamparci? [doh-vay . . . ak-kam-par-chee]

  can we camp here? possiamo accamparci qua?

  camping holiday una vacanza campeggio [va-kan-tzah kam-pay-joh]

  campsite un camping

» TRAVEL TIP: *in Italy you can camp almost anywhere; the best campsites are those recommended by ENIT (the national tourist organization)*

can¹: a can of beer una lattina di birra [. . . dee beer-rah]

  can-opener un apriscatole [a-pree-skah-toh-lay]

can²: can I have . . .? posso avere . . .? [. . . a-vay-ray]

  can you show me . . .? può mostrarmi [pwoh . . . -mee]

  I can't . . . non posso . . .

  he can't . . . non può . . .

  can we . . .? possiamo . . .?

Canada il Canada

Canadian canadese [ka-na-day-say]

cancel: I want to cancel my booking vorrei cancellare la mia prenotazione [vor-ray kan-chel-lah-ray lah mee-ah pray-no-ta-tzee-oh-nay]

  can we cancel dinner for tonight? possiamo cancellare la cena per stasera? [. . . chay-nah . . . sta-say-rah]

candle una candela [-day-lah]

by candlelight al lume di candela [loo-may dee . . .]
capsize capovolgersi [ka-po-vol-jer-see]
car l'auto [ow-toh], la macchina [mak-kee-nah]
  by car in macchina
carafe una caraffa
caravan la roulotte [–lot]
carburettor il carburatore [–toh-ray]
cards le carte [kar-tay]
  do you play cards? gioca a carte? [jo-kah . . .]
care: will you take care of this for me? può prendersi cura di questo per me? [pwoh pren-der-see koo-rah dee kwes-toh payr may]
careful: be careful sta attento
car-ferry il traghetto [tra-ghet-toh]
car park un parcheggio [par-kay-joh]
carpet il tappeto (wall-to-wall) la moquette [–ket]
carrot la carota
carry: will you carry this for me? mi può portare questo? [mee pwoh por-tah-ray . . .]
  carry-cot la culla portatile [kool-lah por-ta-tee-lay]
carving un intaglio [een-tal-yoh]
case (suitcase) una valigia [va-lee-jah]
casello a . . . motorway toll at . . .
cash (money) soldi [sol-dee]
  I haven't any cash non l'ho di moneta [. . . lo dee mo-nay-tah]
  cash desk la cassa
  will you cash a cheque for me? può riscuotere un assegno per me? [pwoh rees-kwoh-tay-ray oon as-sayn-yoh payr may]
casino il casinò [ka-see-noh]
» *TRAVEL TIP: it is important to stress the last syllable; pronounced as in English the word means brothel*
cassa cash point; cashier
cassette una cassetta

....

castle il castello
cat il gatto
catch: where do we catch the bus? dove si
  prende l'autobus? [doh-vay see pren-day
  low-toh-boos]
  he's caught a bug si è preso un malanno [see
  eh pray-soh . . .]
cathedral la cattedrale [–drah-lay]
catholic cattolico [kat-toh-lee-koh]
cauliflower il cavolfiore [–oh-ray]
cave la grotta
ceiling il soffitto
celery il sedano [seh-da-noh]
cellophane il cellophane [chel-lo-fa-nay]
centigrade centigradi [chen-tee-gra-dee]
» TRAVEL TIP: to convert C to F: $\frac{C}{5} \times 9 + 32 = F$

| centigrade | −5 | 0 | 10 | 15 | 21 | 30 | 36.9 |
| Fahrenheit | 23 | 32 | 50 | 59 | 70 | 86 | 98.4 |

centimetre un centimetro [chen-tee-may-troh]
» TRAVEL TIP: 1 cm = 0.39 inches
central centrale [chen-trah-lay]
  with central heating con riscaldamento
  centrale
centre il centro [chen-troh]
  how do we get to the centre? come si va in
  centro? [koh-may see . . .]
certain certo [chayr-toh]
  are you certain? è certo? [eh . . .]
certificate il certificato [cher-tee-fee-kah-toh]
chain la catena [ka-tay-nah]
chair la sedia [seh-dee-ah]
chairlift la seggiovia [seh-jo-vee-ah]
chambermaid la cameriera
  [ka-may-ree-eh-rah]
champagne lo champagne [shom-pan-yuh]
change: could you change this into lire? può
  cambiare questi in lire? [pwoh
  kam-bee-ah-ray . . .]

I haven't any change non ho moneta
[. . . o mo-n*ay*-tah]
do we have to change trains? dobbiamo
cambiare treno?
I'll just get changed vado a cambiarmi
» *TRAVEL TIP: don't be surprised if instead of small*
change you get chewing gum or sweets when
shopping or in a bar!
» *TRAVEL TIP: changing money: as well as banks*
look for 'Agenzia di Cambio'
channel: the Channel la Manica
[m*a*h-nee-kah]
charge: what do you charge? quanto fate
pagare? [. . . f*a*h-tay pa-*gah*-ray]
who's in charge? chi è l'incaricato? [kee
eh . . .]
chart la carta
cheap a buon mercato [ah bwon mayr-k*a*h-toh]
something cheaper qualcosa di meno caro
[. . . dee m*ay*-noh . . .]
cheat: I've been cheated sono stato
imbrogliato [. . . st*a*h-toh eem-brol-y*a*h-toh]
check: will you check? può controllare?
[pwoh . . . –*a*h-ray]
I'm sure, I've checked sono sicuro, ho
controllato [. . . o . . .]
will you check the total? può controllare il
totale [. . . –lay]
we checked in ci siamo registrati [chee . . .]
we checked out abbiamo pagato il conto
cheek la guancia [gw*a*n-chah]
cheeky sfacciato [sfa-ch*a*h-toh]
cheerio ciao [chow]
(toast) cin cin [cheen cheen]
cheers salute [–tay] *(thank you)* grazie
[gr*a*h-tzee-ay]
cheese il formaggio [for-m*a*h-joh]
chef lo chef
chemist's la farmacia [far-ma-ch*ee*-ah]

cheque un assegno [as-sayn-yoh]
  will you take a cheque? prende un assegno?
  [pren-day . . .]
  cheque book il libretto di assegni
  [. . . dee . . .]
  cheque card il cheque card
chest il petto [pet-toh]
» *TRAVEL TIP: chest measurements*

UK	34	36	38	40	42	44	46
Italy	87	91	97	102	107	112	117

chewing gum la gomma da masticare
  [–kah-ray]
chicken il pollo
chickenpox la varicella [va-ree-chel-lah]
child il bambino [bam-bee-noh]
  children i bambini [ee bam-bee-nee]
  children's portion una porzione per bambini
  [. . . por-tzee-oh-nay . . .]
chin il mento
china la porcellana [por-chel-lah-nah]
chips le patatine fritte [lay pa-ta-tee-nay
  freet-tay]
  (casino) le fiches [lay feesh]
chiuso closed
chocolate il cioccolato [chok-ko-lah-toh]
  hot chocolate la cioccolata calda
  a box of chocolates una scatola di
  cioccolatini [skah-toh-lah dee . . .]
choke *(car)* la valvola dell'aria [val-vo-lah
  del-lah-ree-ah]
chop *(noun)* una cotoletta
Christmas Natale [na-tah-lay]
  happy Christmas! buon Natale! [bwon . . .]
church la chiesa [kee-ay-sah]
  where is the Protestant/Catholic church?
  dov'è la chiesa protestante/cattolica?
  [doh-veh . . . pro-tes-tan-tay/kat-toh-lee-kah]
cider il sidro [see-droh]
cigar il sigaro [see-ga-roh]

cigarette una sigaretta
   would you like a cigarette? vuole una
   sigaretta? [vw*oh*-lay . . .]
cine-camera la cinepresa [chee-nay-pr*a*y-sah]
cinema il cinema [ch*ee*-nay-mah]
circle il circolo [ch*ee*r-ko-loh]
   (in cinema) la galleria [*–ee*-ah]
city la città [cheet-t*a*h]
claim *(noun: insurance)* la domanda
   d'indennizzo [. . . deen-den-n*ee*t-tzoh]
clarify chiarire [kee-a-r*ee*-ray]
clean *(adjective)* pulito [poo-l*ee*-toh]
   can I have some clean sheets? posso avere le
   lenzuola pulite? [. . . a-v*a*y-ray lay
   layn-tzwo-lah . . .]
   my room hasn't been cleaned today la mia
   stanza non è stata pulita oggi [m*ee*-ah
   st*a*n-tzah . . . eh . . . *o*-jee]
   it's not clean non è pulito
cleansing cream il detergente [*–*tay]
clear: I'm not clear about it non è chiaro
   [. . . eh kee-*a*h-roh]
clever intelligente [*–*tay]
climate il clima [kl*ee*-mah]
climb: we're going to climb . . . andiamo a
   scalare . . . [. . . ska-l*a*h-ray]
   climber uno scalatore [*–t*oh-ray]
clip *(skiing)* la pinzetta [peen-tz*a*yt-tah]
cloakroom il guardaroba [gwar-da-r*o*-bah]
   (WC) il gabinetto
clock l'orologio [*–o*h-joh]
close[1] vicino [vee-ch*ee*-noh]
   (weather) afoso
close[2]: **when do you close?** quando chiudete?
   [. . . kee-oo-d*a*y-tay]
closed chiuso [kee-*oo*-soh]
cloth la stoffa *(rag)* uno straccio [str*a*h-choh]
clothes i vestiti [ee ves-t*ee*-tee]
cloud la nuvola [n*oo*-vo-lah]

clutch la frizione [free-tzee-*oh*-nay]
  the clutch is slipping la frizione non si [see] innesta
coach la corriera [kor-y*eh*-rah]
coast la costa
  coastguard la guardia costiera [gw*a*r-dee-ah kos-tee-*eh*-rah]
coat il cappotto
cockroach uno scarafaggio [–f*a*dj-yoh]
coffee un caffè [kaf-f*eh*]
  white coffee un cappuccino [kap-poo-ch*ee*-noh]
» *TRAVEL TIP: in Italy coffee is always served black and very strong; if you want it less strong ask for 'un caffè lungo'*
coin una moneta [mo-n*ay*-tah]
cold *(adjective)* freddo
  I'm cold ho freddo [o . . .]
  I've got a cold ho il raffreddore [. . .–d*oh*-ray]
collapse: he's collapsed ha avuto un collasso [ah . . .]
collar il colletto
  collarbone l'osso del collo
» *TRAVEL TIP: collar sizes*

(old) UK	14	14½	15	15½	16	16½	17
continental	36	37	38	39	41	42	43

collect: I want to collect . . . sono venuto a prendere . . . [. . . pr*e*n-day-ray]
colour un colore [ko-l*oh*-ray]
  have you any other colours? avete altri colori? [a-v*a*y-tay . . .]
comb il pettine [p*e*t-tee-nay]
come venire [vay-n*ee*-ray]
  I come from London sono di [dee] Londra
  we came here yesterday siamo arrivati ieri [. . . y*eh*-ree]
  come on! andiamo!
  come with me venga con me [. . . may]
  come here venga qui [. . . kwee]

comfortable comodo [ko-mo-doh]
  it's not very comfortable non è molto comodo
Common Market il Mercato Comune
  [mayr-kah-toh ko-moo-nay]
communication cord il segnale d'allarme
  [sayn-yah-lay dal-lar-may]
company la compagnia [kom-pan-yee-ah]
  you're good company sei simpatico [say
  seem-pah-tee-koh]
compartment (train) uno scompartimento
compass la bussola [boos-so-lah]
compensation un compenso
  I demand compensation voglio un compenso
  [vol-yoh . . .]
complaint una lamentela
  I want to complain about my room vorrei
  sporgere una lamentela a proposito della mia
  stanza [vor-ray spor-jay-ray . . . mee-ah
  stan-tzah]
completely completamente [–mayn-tay]
complicated: it's very complicated è molto
  complicato [eh . . .]
compliment: my compliments to the chef i
  miei complimenti allo chef [ee mee-eh-ee . . .]
concert un concerto [kon-chayr-toh]
concussion la commozione cerebrale
  [. . . –tzee-oh-nay chay-ray-brah-lay]
condition la condizione [–tzee-oh-nay]
  it's not in very good condition non è in
  buone condizioni [. . . eh een bwo-nay . . .]
conference una conferenza [–en-tzah]
confirm confermare [kon-fayr-mah-ray]
confuse: you're confusing me mi confonde
  [mee kon-fon-day]
congratulations! complimenti! [–tee]
conjunctivitis la congiuntivite
  [kon-joon-tee-vee-tay]
connection (rail etc) la coincidenza
  [ko-een-chee-den-tzah]

connoisseur un conoscitore
 [ko-no-shee-*toh*-ray]
conscious conscio [k*o*n-shoh]
consciousness: he's lost consciousness è
 svenuto [eh . . .]
constipation la stitichezza [stee-tee-k*a*yt-tzah]
consul il console [k*o*n-so-lay]
consulate il consolato
contact: how can I contact . . . ? come mi
 metto in contatto con . . . ? [k*oh*-may mee . . .]
 contact lenses le lenti a contatto
contraceptive un contraccettivo
 [kon-tra-chet-*tee*-voh]
convenient conveniente [–en-tay]
cook: it's not cooked è crudo
 it's beautifully cooked è cucinato alla
 perfezione [eh koo-chee-n*ah*-toh *a*l-lah
 per-fay-tzee-*oh*-nay]
 cooker la cucina [koo-ch*ee*-nah]
cool fresco
corkscrew un cavatappi
corn *(foot)* un callo
corner un angolo [*a*n-go-loh]
 can we have a corner table? possiamo avere
 un tavolo d'angolo [. . . a-v*a*y-ray oon
 t*a*h-vo-loh . . .]
cornflakes i [ee] corn flakes
correct corretto
cosmetics i cosmetici [ee kos-m*eh*-tee-chee]
cost: what does it cost? quanto costa?
 that's too much è troppo
 I'll take it lo compro
cotton il cotone [ko-t*oh*-nay]
 cotton wool il cotone idrofilo
 [. . . ee-dro-fee-loh]
couchette la poltrona
cough la tosse [t*o*s-say]
 cough drops le pastiglie per la tosse
 [pas-t*ee*l-yay . . .]

could: could you please . . .? potrebbe . . .?
[po-tray b-bay]
  could I have . . .? potrei avere? [po-tray
a-vay-ray]
country un paese [pa-ay-say]
  in the country in campagna [een
kam-pan-yah]
couple: a couple of . . . un paio di . . . [pah-yoh
dee]
courier la guida [gwee-dah]
course *(of meal)* una portata
  of course certo [chayr-toh]
court: I'll take you to court la cito in tribunale
[lah chee-toh een tree-boo-nah-lay]
cousin un cugino [koo-jee-noh]
cover: keep him well covered lo tenga ben
coperto; **cover charge** il coperto
cow la mucca [mook-kah]
crab il granchio [gran-kee-oh]
crash: there's been a crash c'è stato uno
scontro [cheh stah-toh . . .]
  crash helmet un casco
crazy: you're crazy è pazzo [eh pat-tzoh]
cream la crema *(fresh)* la panna
creche l'asilo nido [a-see-loh nee-doh]
credit card una carta di credito [. . . dee
kreh-dee-toh]
crisis una crisi [kree-see]
crisps le patatine [pa-ta-tee-nay]
crossroads l'incrocio [een-kroh-choh]
crowded affollato
cruise una crociera [kro-chay-rah]
crutch una gruccia [groo-chah]
  (of body) l'inguine [een-gwee-nay]
cry: don't cry non piangere [non
pee-an-jay-ray]
cup una tazza [tat-tzah]
  a cup of coffee una tazza di caffè [. . . dee
kaf-feh]

....

cupboard un armadio [ar-m*ah*-dee-oh]
curry il curry
curtains le tende [t*e*n-day]
cushion il cuscino [koo-sh*ee*-noh]
Customs la Dogana
cut: I've cut myself mi sono tagliato
[mee-s*oh*-noh tal-y*ah*-toh]
cycle: can we cycle there? ci si può andare con
la bicicletta? [chee see pwoh an-d*ah*-ray kon la
bee-chee-kl*ay*t-tah]
cyclist un ciclista [chee-kl*ee*s-tah]
cylinder il cilindro [chee-l*ee*n-droh]
  cylinder head gasket la guarnizione del
  cilindro [gwar-nee-tzee-*oh*-nay . . .]
dad(dy) il papà
damage: I'll pay for the damage pago per il
guasto [gw*as*-toh]
  it's damaged è danneggiato
  [eh dan-nay-j*ah*-toh]
damn! maledizione! [ma-lay-dee-tzee-*oh*-nay]
damp umido [*oo*-mee-doh]
dance: is there a dance on? si balla? [see . . .]
  would you like to dance? vuoi ballare?
  [vw*o*-ee bal-l*ah*-ray]
dangerous pericoloso
dark scuro
  when does it get dark? quando fa buio?
  [. . . b*oo*-yoh]
  dark green verde scuro [v*ay*r-day . . .]
darling tesoro
dashboard il cruscotto
date: what's the date? quanti ne [nay]
abbiamo?
  can we fix a date? possiamo fissare un
  appuntamento? [. . . fees-s*ah*-ray . . .]
  on the first of March il primo marzo
  [pr*ee*-moh m*ar*-tzoh]
  on the fifth of May il cinque maggio
  [ch*ee*n-kway m*ah*-joh]

in 1982 nel millenovecentottantadue
[m*ee*-lay-no-vay-chen-toh-ot-tan-ta-d*oo*-ay]

» *TRAVEL TIP: to say the date just use the ordinary
number as shown above (the exception is 'the
first'); numbers are listed on page 128*

dates *(fruit)* i datteri [ee d*a*t-tay-ree]

daughter: my daughter mia figlia [m*ee*-ah
f*ee*l-yah]

day il giorno [jor-noh]

dazzle: his lights were dazzling me i suoi fari
mi abbagliavano [ee sw*oy*-ee f*a*h-ree mee
ab-bal-y*a*h-va-noh]

dead morto

deaf sordo

deal *(business)* un affare [af-f*a*h-ray]
it's a deal affare fatto
will you deal with it? se ne occupa lei? [say
nay *o*k-koo-pah lay]

dear *(expensive)* caro
Dear Sir Egregio Signore [ay-gr*a*y-joh
seen-y*oh*-ray]
Dear Madam Egregia Signora
Dear Franco Caro Franco

December dicembre [dee-ch*e*m-bray]

deck il ponte [pon-tay]
deckchair una sedia a sdraio [s*e*h-dee-ah ah
sdr*a*h-yoh]

declare: I have nothing to declare non ho
niente da dichiarare [non o nee-*e*n-tay dah
deek-ya-r*a*h-ray]

deep profondo
is it deep? è profondo? [eh . . .]

defendant l'accusato

de-icer l'antighiaccio [an-teeg-y*a*h-choh]

delay: the flight was delayed il volo ha avuto
un ritardo [. . . ah a-v*oo*-toh . . .]

deliberately apposta

delicate *(person)* delicato

delicatessen una salumeria [–may-r*ee*-ah]

....

delicious delizioso [day-lee-tzee-*oh*-soh]
delivery: is there another mail delivery? c'è
    un'altra distribuzione di posta? [cheh . . .
    –tzee-*oh*-nay dee pos-tah]
de luxe di lusso [dee *loos*-soh]
democratic democratico [day-mo-kr*ah*-tee-koh]
dent una ammaccatura
    you've dented my car ha ammaccato la mia
    auto [ah . . . m*ee*-ah *ow*-toh]
dentist il dentista
    YOU MAY HEAR . . .
    apra bene *open wide*
    si sciacqui *please rinse out*
dentures la dentiera [dent-y*ay*-rah]
deny: I deny it lo nego
deodorant il deodorante [–tay]
departure la partenza [par-t*en*-tzah]
depend: it depends (on him) dipende (da lui)
    [dee-p*en*-day dah *loo*-ee]
deport deportare [–t*ah*-ray]
deposit un deposito [day-po-see-toh]
    do I have to leave a deposit? devo lasciare un
    deposito? [d*ay*-voh la-sh*ah*-ray . . .]
deposito bagagli *left luggage*
depressed depresso
depth la profondità [pro-fon-dee-t*ah*]
desperate: I'm desperate for a drink ho una
    sete terribile [o *oo*-nah s*ay*-tay ter-r*ee*-bee-lay]
dessert il dolce [d*ol*-chay]
destination la destinazione [–tzee-*oh*-nay]
detergent il detergente [–j*en*-tay]
detour una deviazione [–tzee-*oh*-nay]
devalued svalutato
develop: could you develop these? può
    sviluppare questi?
    [pwoh svee-loop-p*ah*-ray . . .]
deviazione *diversion*
diabetic un diabetico [dee-a-b*eh*-tee-koh]
dialling code il prefisso

diamond un diamante [–tay]
diarrhoea la diarrea [dee-ar-*ray*-ah]
  have you got something for diarrhoea? ha
  qualcosa per la diarrea? [ah . . .]
diary il diario [dee-*ah*-ree-oh]
dictionary il dizionario [dee-tzee-o-*nah*-ree-oh]
didn't *see* not
die morire [mo-*ree*-ray]
  he's dying sta morendo
diesel *(fuel)* il diesel
diet la dieta [dee-*ay*-tah]
  I'm on a diet sono a dieta
different: they are different sono diversi
  can I have a different room? posso avere
  un'altra camera? [. . . a-*vay*-ray . . .]
  is there a different route? c'è un'altra
  strada? [cheh . . .]
difficult difficile [deef-*fee*-chee-lay]
digestion la digestione [–*oh*-nay]
dinghy il dinghy
dining room la sala da pranzo [. . . pr*a*n-tzoh]
dinner la cena [ch*ay*-nah]
  dinner jacket lo smoking
dipped headlights gli anabbaglianti [lee
  a-nab-bal-y*a*n-tee]
direct *(adjective)* diretto [dee–]
  does it go direct? ci va diretto? [chee . . .]
dirty sporco
disabled invalido [een-v*ah*-lee-doh]
disappear sparire [spa-*ree*-ray]
  it's just disappeared è sparito [eh . . .]
disappointing deludente [–tay]
disco la discoteca
  see you in the disco ci vediamo in discoteca
  [chee . . .]
discount lo sconto
disgusting disgustoso
dish un piatto [pee-*at*-toh]
dishonest disonesto

....

disinfectant un disinfettante [–tay], l'alcol
» *TRAVEL TIP: the latter, which is pure alcohol,*
  usually pink in colour, is the standard
  disinfectant
dispensing chemist la farmacia
  [far-ma-ch*ee*-ah]
distance: in the distance in lontananza
  [een lon-ta-n*a*n-tzah]
distress signal un segnale di soccorso
  [sayn-y*ah*-lay dee . . .]
distributor *(car)* lo spinterogeno
  [speen-tay-ro-jay-noh]
disturb: the noise is disturbing me il rumore
  mi disturba [eel roo-m*oh*-ray mee
  dees-t*oo*r-bah]
divieto di . . . do not . . .
divorced divorziato [dee-vor-tzee-*ah*-toh]
do: how do you do? piacere [pee-a-ch*ay*-ray]
  what are you doing tonight? cosa fa stasera?
  how do you do it? come fa? [k*oh*-may fah]
  will you do it for me? lo può fare lei? [loh
  pwoh f*ah*-ray lay]
  I've never done it before non l'ho mai fatto
  prima [non lo m*ah*-ee f*a*t-toh pr*ee*-mah]
  I was doing 60 kph andavo a sessanta all'ora
doctor il medico [m*eh*-dee-koh]
  I need a doctor ho bisogno di un medico
  [o bee-sonn-yoh dee . . .]
» *TRAVEL TIP: any chemist (farmacia) will have a*
  list of the nearest doctors
  YOU MAY HEAR . . .
  l'è mai successo prima? *have you had this*
  before?
  dove le fa male? *where does it hurt?*
  sta prendendo delle medicine? *are you taking*
  any drugs?
  ne prenda una/due . . . *take one/two . . .*
  una volta/due volte/tre volte al giorno
  once/twice/three times a day

document il documento
dog il cane [k*ah*-nay]
dogana customs
don't! no!; *see* **not**
door la porta
dosage la dose [d*oh*-say]
double: double room una camera a due letti
[k*ah*-may-rah ah d*oo*-ay let-teeh]
(with double bed) una camera matrimoniale
[–ee-*ah*-lay]
double whisky un whisky doppio
[. . . d*o*p-pee-oh]
down: get down! giù! [joo]
downstairs dabbasso
it's just down the road è qui vicino [eh kwee
vee-ch*ee*-noh]
drain il tubo di scarico [t*oo*-boh dee
sk*ah*-ree-koh]
drawing pin una puntina [poon-t*ee*-nah]
dress un vestito [ves-t*ee*-toh]
dressing gown una vestaglia [ves-t*a*l-yah]
» *TRAVEL TIP: sizes*

UK	10	12	14	16	18	20
Italy	38	40	42	44	46	48

dressing *(for wound)* la medicazione
[may-dee-ka-tzee-*oh*-nay]
(for salad) il condimento
drink: would you like something to drink?
vuole bere qualcosa? [vw*oh*-lay b*a*y-ray . . .]
I don't drink non bevo alcolici [. . . b*a*y-voh
al-k*oh*-lee-chee]
is the water drinkable? l'acqua è
potabile? [. . . eh po-t*ah*-bee-lay]
drive guidare [gwee-d*ah*-ray]
I've been driving all day è tutto il giorno che
guido [eh t*oo*t-toh eel jor-noh kay . . .]
driver l'autista [low-t*ee*s-tah]
driving licence la patente [pa-t*e*n-tay]
drown: he's drowning sta annegando

drug la droga
drunk ubriaco [oo-bree-*ah*-koh]
dry *(adjective)* asciutto [a-sh*oo*t-toh]
  (wine) secco
  dry-cleaner's un lavasecco
due: when is the bus due? quando arriva
  l'autobus? [. . . *low*-toh-boos]
during durante [doo-r*a*n-tay]
dust la polvere [p*o*l-vay-ray]
duty-free *(noun)* il duty-free
dynamo la dinamo [*dee*-na-moh]
each: can we have one each? possiamo averne
  uno ciascuno [. . . a-v*a*yr-nay *oo*-noh
  chas-k*oo*-noh]
  how much are they each? quanto costano
  l'uno?
ear l'orecchio [or-r*a*yk-yoh]
  I have earache ho il mal d'orecchi [o . . .]
early presto
  we want to leave a day earlier vogliamo
  partire un giorno prima [vol-y*ah*-moh
  par-*tee*-ray oon jor-noh pr*ee*-mah]
  early closing la chiusura anticipata
  [kee-oo-*soo*-rah an-tee-chee-p*ah*-tah]
earring l'orecchino [o-rayk-*kee*-noh]
east est
Easter Pasqua [p*a*s-kwah]
easy facile [f*ah*-chee-lay]
eat mangiare [man-j*ah*-ray]
  something to eat qualcosa da mangiare
egg un uovo [w*o*-voh]
Eire l'Irlanda
either: either . . . or . . . o . . . o . . .
  I don't like either non mi piace nessuno dei
  due [non mee pee-*ah*-chay nes-*soo*-noh day
  d*oo*-ay]
elastic elastico [ay-l*a*s-tee-koh]
  elastic band un elastico
elbow il gomito [g*o*-mee-toh]

electric elettrico [ay-let-tree-koh]
  electric blanket la coperta elettrica
  electric fire la stufetta elettrica
electrician l'elettricista [ay-layt-tree-chees-tah]
electricity l'elettricità [ay-layt-tree-chee-tah]
elegant elegante [. . .–tay]
else: something else qualcosa d'altro
  somewhere else da qualche altra parte
  [dah-kwal-kay al-trah par-tay]
  who else? chi altro? [kee . . .]
  or else o altrimenti
embarrassed imbarazzato
  [eem-ba-rat-tzah-toh]
embarrassing imbarazzante
  [eem-ba-rat-tzan-tay]
embassy l'ambasciata [am-ba-shah-tah]
emergency emergenza [ay-mayr-jen-tzah]
empty vuoto [vwo-toh]
enclose: I enclose . . . accludo . . .
end la fine [fee-nay]
  when does it end? quando finisce . . .?
  [. . . fee-nee-shay]
engaged *(telephone, toilet)* occupato
  (person) fidanzato [fee-dan-tzah-toh]
engagement ring anello di fidanzamento
  [. . . dee fee-dan-tza-men-toh]
engine il motore [mo-toh-ray]
  engine trouble un guasto al motore
  [gwas-toh . . .]
England l'Inghilterra [een-gheel-ter-rah]
English inglese [een-glay-say]
  the English gli Inglesi [lee . . .]
  do you speak English? parla l'inglese?
enjoy: I enjoyed it very much mi è piaciuto
  molto [mee eh pee-a-choo-toh mol-toh]
enlargement *(photo)* un ingrandimento
enormous enorme [ay-nor-may]
enough: thank you, that's enough basta,
  grazie [. . . grah-tzee-ay]

....

entertainment il divertimento [dee-vayr-tee–]
entrance l'entrata
entrata *entrance*
entry l'entrata
envelope una busta [boos-tah]
equipment l'equipaggiamento
  [ay-kwee-pa-ja-men-toh]
error un errore [ayr-roh-ray]
escalator la scala mobile [. . . mo-bee-lay]
especially specialmente [spay-chal-men-tay]
essential essenziale [es-sen-tzee-ah-lay]
  it is essential that . . . è indispensabile che . . .
  [eh een-dees-pen-sah-bee-lay kay]
evacuate evacuare [–ray]
even: even the British perfino gli Inglesi
  [per-fee-noh lee een-glay-see]
evening la sera [say-rah]
  this evening stasera
  in the evening la sera
  good evening buona sera [bwo-nah . . .]
  evening dress l'abito da sera [ah-bee-toh . . .]
ever: have you ever been to . . .? è mai stato
  a . . .? [eh mah-ee . . .]
every ogni [on-yee]
  every day ogni giorno [. . . jor-noh]
everyone tutti [toot-tee]
  everything tutto
  everywhere dappertutto
exact esatto
example esempio [ay-sem-pee-oh]
  for example per esempio
excellent eccellente [ay-chayl-len-tay]
except: except me eccetto me [ay-chet-toh
  may]
excess eccesso [ay-ches-soh]
  excess baggage bagaglio eccedente
  [ba-gal-yoh ay-chay-den-tay]
exchange *(money)* cambio [kam-bee-oh]
  (telephone) il centralino [chen-tra-lee-noh]

exciting entusiasmante [–tay]
  how exciting! che bello! [kay . . .]
excursion una gita [jee-tah]
excuse me *(to get past)* permesso
  (to get attention) scusi [skoo-zee]
  (apology) mi scusi [mee . . .]
exhaust *(car)* lo scappamento
exhausted sfinito [sfee-nee-toh]
exhibition un'esposizione
  [ays-po-see-tzee-oh-nay]
exhibitor un espositore [–ray]
exit l'uscita [oo-shee-tah]
expect: she's expecting è incinta [eh
  een-cheen-tah]
expenses: it's on expenses è a spese della ditta
  [eh ah spay-say del-lah deet-tah]
expensive costoso
expert esperto
explain spiegare [spee-ay-gah-ray]
  would you explain that slowly? può
  spiegarlo lentamente? [pwoh spee-ay-gar-loh
  len-ta-men-tay]
export *(noun)* l'esportazione
  [ays-por-ta-tzee-oh-nay]
exposure meter l'esposimetro
  [ays-po-see-may-troh]
express espresso
extra *(adjective):* **an extra day** un altro giorno
  is that extra? è extra? [eh . . .]
extremely estremamente [–tay]
eye l'occhio [ok-yoh]
  eyebrow il sopracciglio [so-pra-cheel-yoh]
  eyeshadow l'ombretto
  eye witness un testimone oculare
  [tes-tee-moh-nay o-koo-lah-ray]
F *(on tap)* cold
face la faccia [fah-chah]
  face mask *(diving)* la maschera
  [mas-kay-rah]

fact il fatto
factory la fabbrica [fab-bree-kah]
Fahrenheit il Fahrenheit

» *TRAVEL TIP: to convert F to C:* $F - 32 \times \frac{5}{9} = C$

Fahrenheit	23	32	50	59	70	86	98.4
centigrade	−5	0	10	15	21	30	36.9

faint: she's fainted è svenuta [eh . . .]
fair una fiera [fee-ay-rah]
  that's not fair non è giusto [. . . eh joos-toh]
faithfully: yours faithfully distinti saluti
fake falso
fall: he's fallen è caduto [eh . . .]
false falso
  false teeth i denti finti [den-tee feen-tee]
family la famiglia [fa-meel-yah]
fan il ventilatore [ven-tee-la-toh-ray]
  (hand-held) un ventaglio [ven-tal-yoh]
  (football etc) un tifoso [tee–]
  fan-belt la cinghia [cheen-ghee-ah]
far lontano
  is it far? è lontano? [eh . . .]
  how far is it? quanto dista? [. . . dees-tah]
fare *(travel)* (il prezzo del) biglietto [pret-tzoh
  dayl beel-yet-toh]
farm la fattoria [fat-toh-ree-ah]
farther più lontano [pew . . .]
fashion la moda
fast veloce [vay-loh-chay]
  don't speak so fast non parli così in fretta
  [. . . ko-see . . .]
fat grasso
fatally fatalmente [–tay]
father: my father mio padre [mee-oh pah-dray]
fathom un braccio [brah-choh]
fault un difetto
  it's not my fault non è colpa mia [. . . mee-ah]
faulty difettoso
favourite favorito [fa-vo-ree-toh]

February febbraio [feb-bra*h*-yoh]
fed-up: I'm fed-up sono stufo [. . . st*oo*-foh]
feel: I feel cold/hot ho freddo/caldo [o . . .]
   I feel sad sono triste [. . . tr*ee*s-tay]
   I feel like . . . ho voglia di . . . [o v*o*l-yah dee]
ferry il traghetto [tra-g*ay*t-toh]
fetch: will you come and fetch me? mi viene a
   prendere? [mee vee-*ay*-nay ah pr*e*n-day-ray]
fever la febbre [f*e*b-bray]
few: only a few solo pochi [p*o*-kee]
   a few days pochi giorni [po-kee j*o*r-nee]
fiancé(e) fidanzato (fidanzata)
   [fee-dan-tz*ah*-toh . . .]
fiddle: it's a fiddle è un imbroglio [eh oon
   eem-brol-yoh]
field un campo
figs i fichi [ee f*ee*-kee]
figure *(number)* una cifra [ch*ee*-frah]
   I'm watching my figure sto attenta alla linea
   [. . . l*ee*-nay-ah]
fill: fill her up mi faccia il pieno [mee f*ah*-chah
   eel pee-*eh*-noh]
   to fill in a form riempire un modulo
   [ree-aym-p*ee*-ray oon m*o*-doo-loh]
fillet il filetto
film *(movie)* un film [feelm]
   do you have this type of film? avete questo
   tipo di pellicola? [a-v*ay*-tay kwes-toh t*ee*-poh
   dee payl-l*ee*-ko-lah]
filter un filtro
   filter/non-filter col filtro/senza filtro
find trovare [tro-v*ah*-ray]
   if you find it . . . se lo trova . . . [say . . .]
   I've found a . . . ho trovato un . . . [o . . .]
fine: fine weather bel tempo
   a 50,000 lire fine una multa di cinquanta mila
   lire [m*oo*l-tah dee cheen-kw*a*n-tah m*ee*-lah
   l*ee*-ray]
finger un dito [d*ee*-toh]

fingernail l'unghia [*oon*-ghee-ah]
finish: I haven't finished non ho finito [non o fee-*nee*-toh]
fire: fire! al fuoco! [*fwo*-koh]
  can we light a fire here? possiamo accendere un fuoco qui? [. . . a-chen-day-ray oon fwo-koh kwee]
  it's not firing *(car)* non si accende [non see a-chen-day]
  fire brigade i vigili del fuoco [ee vee-jee-lee del fwo-koh]
  fire extinguisher un estintore [ays-teen-*toh*-ray]
» *TRAVEL TIP: in the event of a fire phone 113*
first primo [*pree*-moh]
  I was first c'ero prima io [ch*eh*-roh pr*ee*-mah *ee*-oh]
  first aid il pronto soccorso
  first aid kit la cassetta di [dee] pronto soccorso
  first class di prima classe [dee pr*ee*-mah kl*a*s-say]
  first name il nome di battesimo [n*oh*-may dee bat-*tay*-see-moh]
fish il pesce [p*ay*-shay]
fishing la pesca
  fishing rod la canna da pesca
five cinque [ch*ee*n-kway]
fix: can you fix it? *(repair)* può ripararlo? [pwoh ree-pa-r*ar*-loh]
fizzy gassato
flag la bandiera [ban-dee-*ay*-rah]
flash *(photo)* il flash
flat *(apartment)* un appartamento *(adjective)* piatto [pee-*at*-toh]
  this drink is flat questa bibita è svanita [. . . b*ee*-bee-tah eh sva-n*ee*-tah]
  I've got a flat (tyre) ho una foratura [o*oo*-nah fo-ra-*too*-rah]
flavour il sapore [sa-p*oh*-ray]

flea la pulce [pool-chay]
flies *(trousers)* la cerniera [chayr-nee-*ay*-rah]
flight il volo
flippers le pinne [lay-peen-nay]
flirt *(verb)* flirtare [fleer-*tah*-ray]
float *(verb)* galleggiare [gal-lay-j*ah*-ray]
floor il pavimento
  on the second floor al secondo piano
flower un fiore [fee-*oh*-ray]
flu l'influenza [een-floo-*e*n-tzah]
fly *(insect)* una mosca
foggy nebbioso
follow seguire [say-gwee-ray]
food il cibo [ch*ee*-boh] *see pages 70–71*
  food poisoning avvelenamento da cibo
fool uno sciocco [shok-koh]
foot il piede [pee-*ay*-day]
» *TRAVEL TIP: 1 foot = 30.1 cm = 0.3 metres*
football *(game)* il calcio [k*a*l-choh]
for per [payr]
forbidden vietato [vee-ay-t*ah*-toh]
foreign straniero [stran-y*eh*-roh]
  foreign exchange il cambio estero
  [k*a*m-bee-oh *e*s-tay-roh]
foreigner uno straniero [stran-y*eh*-roh]
forget dimenticare [dee-men-tee-k*ah*-ray]
  I forget, I've forgotten non mi ricordo
  don't forget non dimenticare
  I'll never forget you non ti dimenticherò mai
  [non tee dee-men-tee-kay-ro m*ah*-ee]
fork la forchetta [for-k*ay*t-tah]
form *(document)* un modulo [mo-doo-loh]
formal formale [for-m*ah*-lay]
fortnight due settimane [d*oo*-ay
  sayt-tee-m*ah*-nay]
forward *(adverb)* avanti
  could you forward my mail? può inoltrare la
  mia posta? [pwoh ee-nol-tr*ah*-ray la
  m*ee*-ah-pos-tah]

foundation cream il fondotinta
fracture una frattura [frat-*too*-rah]
fragile fragile [fr*ah*-jee-lay]
France la Francia [fr*a*n-chah]
free libero [*lee*-bay-roh] *(no charge)* gratis
  admission free ingresso libero
freight *(goods)* le merci [m*a*yr-chee]
French francese [fran-ch*a*y-say]
freshen up: I want to freshen up vorrei darmi
  una rinfrescata [vor-r*a*y d*a*r-mee . . .]
Friday venerdì [vay-nayr-d*ee*]
fridge il frigo [fr*ee*-goh]
friend un amico [a-m*ee*-koh]
friendly cordiale [kor-dee-*ah*-lay]
from da
  where is it from? da dove viene? [dah
  d*oh*-vay vee-*a*y-nay]
front *(noun)* il davanti
  in front of you davanti a lei [. . . lay]
  at the front davanti
frost il gelo [j*a*y-loh]
  frostbite il congelamento
  [kon-jay-la-m*e*n-toh]
frozen congelato [kon-jay-l*ah*-toh]
fruit la frutta
  fruit salad una macedonia [ma-chay-d*o*n-yah]
fry friggere [fr*ee*-jay-ray]
  nothing fried niente di fritto [nee-*e*n-tay dee
  fr*ee*t-toh]
  fried egg un uovo fritto [w*o*-voh . . .]
  frying pan una padella
fuel il combustibile [kom-boos-t*ee*-bee-lay]
full pieno [pee-*a*y-noh]
fun: it's fun è divertente [eh dee-vayr-t*e*n-tay]
funny *(comical)* buffo [b*oo*f-foh]
  (strange) strano [str*ah*-noh]
furniture il mobilio [mo-b*ee*l-yoh]
further *(adverb)* oltre [*o*l-tray]
fuse un fusibile [foo-*see*-bee-lay]

future il futuro [foo-*too*-roh]
  in future in futuro
gabinetti *toilets*
gale una bufera [boo-*fay*-rah]
galleria *tunnel*
gallon un gallone [–nay]
» *TRAVEL TIP: 1 gallon = 4.55 litres*
gallstone un calcolo [k*a*l-ko-loh]
gamble *(verb)* giocare d'azzardo [jo-k*a*h-ray
  dat-t*za*r-doh]
gammon il prosciutto affumicato [pro-sh*oo*t-toh
  af-foo-mee-k*a*h-toh]
garage il garage [ga-*rah*-jay]
» *TRAVEL TIP: Italian garages tend to close between
  1.00 and 3.00 pm*
garden il giardino [jar-d*ee*-noh]
garlic l'aglio [*a*l-yoh]
gas il gas *(petrol)* la benzina [ben-t*zee*-nah]
  gas cooker una cucina a gas
  [koo-ch*ee*-nah . . .]
  gas cylinder la bombola del gas
  [b*o*m-bo-lah . . .]
gasket la guarnizione [gwar-nee-tzee-*oh*-nay]
gay *(homosexual)* omosessuale
  [o-mo-ses-soo-*ah*-lay]
gear la marcia [m*a*r-chah]
  (equipment) l'attrezzatura [at-tray-tza-*too*-rah]
  gearbox la scatola del cambio [sk*a*h-toh-lah
  del k*a*m-bee-oh]
  gear lever la leva del cambio [*lay*-vah . . .]
  I can't get it into gear non riesco ad innestare
  la marcia [non ree-*ays*-koh ad een-nes-
  t*a*h-ray . . .]
gents *(toilet)* uomini
» *TRAVEL TIP: only written: ask for* la toilette
  [twa-l*e*t]
German tedesco
Germany la Germania [jayr-m*a*n-yah]
gesture un gesto [j*e*s-toh]

get: will you get me a . . .? mi può prendere
un . . .? [mee pwoh pren-day-ray oon . . .]
how do I get to . . .? come faccio per andare
a . . .? [koh-may fah-choh payr an-dah-ray
ah . . .]
when can I get it back? quando me [may] lo
ritorna?
where do I get off? dove scendo? [doh-vay
shen-doh]
when do we get back? quando torniamo?
where can I get a bus for . . .? dove posso
prendere un autobus per . . .?
have you got . . .? ha . . .? [ah]
gin il gin
gin and tonic un gin and tonic
girl una ragazza [ra-gat-tzah]
my girlfriend la mia ragazza [mee-ah . . .]
give dare [dah-ray]
will you give me . . .? mi dà . . .? [mee . . .]
I gave it to him gliel'ho dato [lee-ay-lo . . .]
glad contento
glandular fever la febbre ghiandolare [feb-bray
ghee-an-doh-lah-ray]
glass il vetro
a glass un bicchiere [beek-yeh-ray]
glasses gli occhiali [ok-yah-lee]
gloves i guanti [ee gwan-tee]
glue la colla
go: can I have a go? posso provare?
[. . . pro-vah-ray]
my car won't go la mia macchina non parte
[lah mee-ah mak-kee-nah non par-tay]
when does the bus go? quando parte
l'autobus? [kwan-doh par-tay low-toh-boos]
where are you going? dove vai? [doh-vay
vah-ee]
the bus has gone l'autobus è partito
he's gone è andato via [eh . . . vee-ah]
goal *(football)* un goal

goat la capra
god il dio [d*ee*-oh]
goggles *(skiing)* gli occhiali da neve [lee
  ok-y*ah*-lee da n*ay*-vay]
gold l'oro
golf il golf
good buono [bw*o*-noh]
  good! bene! [b*ay*-nay]
goodbye arrivederci [ar-ree-vay-d*ayr*-chee]
gooseberries uva spina [*oo*-vah sp*ee*-nah]
gramme un grammo
» *TRAVEL TIP: 100 grammes = approx 3½ oz*
grand grandioso [gran-dee-*oh*-soh]
  grandfather il nonno
  grandmother la nonna
  my grandson/granddaughter mio
  nipote/mia nipote [m*ee*-oh
  nee-p*oh*-tay/m*ee*-ah . . .]
grapes l'uva [*oo*-vah]
grapefruit il pompelmo
  grapefruit juice il succo di pompelmo
  [s*oo*k-koh dee]
grass l'erba [*er*-bah]
grateful grato [gr*ah*-toh]
  I'm very grateful to you le sono molto grato
  [lay . . .]
gravy il sugo [s*oo*-goh]
grease il grasso *(car etc)* il lubrificante
  [loo-bree-fee-k*a*n-tay]
greasy unto [*oon*-toh]
great *(big)* grande [. . . day] *(very good)*
  bellissimo
  great! benissimo!
greedy ingordo [een-g*or*-doh]
green verde [v*ayr*-day]
  greengrocer's il fruttivendolo
  [froot-tee-ven-doh-loh]
  green card la carta verde
grey grigio [gr*ee*-joh]

....

grilled alla griglia [. . . gr**ee**l-yah]
grocer's una drogheria [dro-gay-r**ee**-ah]
ground: on the ground a terra
  on the ground floor a pian terreno [ah pee-*a*n tayr-r*ay*-noh]
group un gruppo [gr**oo**p-poh]
  our group leader il nostro capogruppo
  I'm with the English group sono con il gruppo degli Inglesi [dayl-yee een-gl*ay*-see]
guarantee: is there a guarantee? ha la garanzia? [ah lah ga-ran-tz**ee**-ah]
guasto **out of order**
guest l'ospite [*o*s-pee-tay]
guesthouse una pensione [payn-see-*oh*-nay]
guide una guida [gw**ee**-dah]
guilty colpevole [kol-p*ay*-vo-lay]
guitar una chitarra [kee-t*a*r-rah]
gums *(in mouth)* le gengive [jen-j**ee**-vay]
gun una pistola [pees-t*oh*-lah]
gynaecologist il ginecologo [jee-nay-k*o*-lo-goh]
hair i capelli *(plural)* [ee . . .]
  hairbrush una spazzola per capelli [sp*a*t-tzo-lah . . .]
  where can I get a haircut? dove posso farmi tagliare i capelli? [d*oh*-vay p*o*s-soh f*a*r-mee tal-y*ah*-ray . . .]
  is there a hairdresser's here? c'è un parrucchiere qui? [cheh oon par-rook-y*ay*-ray kwee]
  hairgrip una molletta
half una metà [may-t*ah*]
  a half portion una mezza porzione [m*e*t-tzah por-tzee-*oh*-nay]
  half an hour mezz'ora
ham il prosciutto [pro-sh**oo**t-toh]
  hamburger un hamburger
hammer un martello
hand la mano
  handbag la borsetta [bor-s*a*yt-tah]

handbrake il freno a mano
handkerchief il fazzoletto [fat-tzoh-*lay*t-toh]
handle *(door)* la maniglia [ma-*nee*l-yah]
   (cup) il manico [*mah*-nee-koh]
hand luggage il bagaglio a mano
   [ba-*gal*-yoh . . .]
handmade lavorato a mano
handsome bello
hanger la gruccia [*groo*-chah]
hangover il mal di [dee] capo (dopo una sbornia)
   my head is killing me mi scoppia la testa
happen accadere [ak-ka-*day*-ray]
   I don't know how it happened non so come è
   successo [. . . *koh*-may eh soo-*ches*-soh]
   what's happening/happened? cosa
   succede/è successo? [. . . soo-*chay*-day . . .]
happy contento
harbour il porto
hard duro [*doo*-roh]
   hard-boiled egg uovo sodo [wo-voh . . .]
   push hard spinga forte [sp*ee*n-gah for-tay]
harm il male [*mah*-lay]
hat il cappello
hate: I hate . . . odio . . . [*o*-dee-oh]
have avere [a-*vay*-ray]
   I have a pain ho un dolore [o oon doh-*loh*-ray]
   do you have any cigars/a map? ha dei
   sigari/una pianta? [ah day *see*-ga-ree . . .]
   can I have some water/some more? posso
   avere dell'acqua/averne ancora?
   [. . . a-v*ay*r-nay an-k*oh*-rah]
   I have to leave tomorrow devo partire
   domani [d*ay*-voh par-*tee*-ray doh-m*ah*-nee]
hayfever la febbre da fieno [*f*eb-bray dah
   fee-*ay*-noh]
he lui [*loo*-ee]
   he is è [eh]
   where does he live? dove abita? [d*oh*-vay
   ah-bee-tah]

head la testa
  headache il mal di testa [. . . dee . . .]
  headlight il faro [*fah*-roh]
  head waiter il capocameriere
  [ka-po-ka-mayr-*yeh*-ray]
  head wind un vento di prua [. . . dee pr*oo*-ah]
health la salute [sa-*loo*-tay]
  your health! salute!
healthy sano
hear: I can't hear non sento
  hearing aid un apparecchio acustico
  [ap-pa-r*ay*k-yoh a-k*oos*-tee-koh]
heart il cuore [kw*o*-ray]
  heart attack un colpo al cuore
heat il calore [ka-*loh*-ray]
  heat stroke un colpo di calore [. . . dee . . .]
heating il riscaldamento
heavy pesante [pay-s*a*n-tay]
heel il calcagno [kal-k*a*n-yoh]
  (on shoe) il tacco
  could you put new heels on these? può
  mettere i tacchi a questi? [pwoh m*e*t-tay-ray ee
  t*a*k-kee . . .]
hello ciao [chow]
help *(noun)* aiuto [a-*yoo*-toh]
  can you help me? mi può aiutare? [mee pwoh
  a-yoo-t*ah*-ray]
  help! aiuto!
her lei [lay]
  have you seen her? l'ha vista? [lah . . .]
  will you give it to her? vuole darglielo?
  [vw*o*h-lay d*a*r-lee-ay-loh]
  it's her bag/plate è la sua borsa/il suo piatto
  it's hers è sua/suo
here qui [kwee]
high alto
hill la collina [kol-*lee*-nah]
  up/down the hill in salita/discesa [een
  sa-*lee*-tah/dee-sh*ay*-sah]

him lui [*loo*-ee]
  I know him lo conosco
  will you give it to him? vuole darglielo?
  [vw*oh*-lay d*a*r-lee-ay-loh]
hire *see* **rent**
his il suo [*soo*-oh]; la sua
  (plural) i suoi [ee sw*oy*-ee]; le sue [–ay]
  it's his è il suo/la sua [eh . . .]
hit: he hit me mi ha colpito [mee ah kol-p*ee*-toh]
hitch-hike *(verb)* fare l'autostop [f*a*h-ray
  low-toh-st*o*p]
  hitch-hiker un autostoppista
  [ow-toh-stop-p*ee*s-tah]
hold tenere [tay-n*a*y-ray]
hole un buco [*boo*-koh]
holiday una vacanza [va-k*a*n-tzah]
  I'm on holiday sono in vacanza
home la casa [k*a*h-sah]
  I want to go home voglio andare a casa
  [vol-yoh an-d*a*h-ray . . .]
  at home a casa
  I am homesick ho nostalgia di casa
  [o nos-tal-j*ee*-ah dee . . .]
honest onesto
  honestly? davvero?
honey il miele [mee-*ay*-lay]
honeymoon la luna di miele [. . . dee . . .]
hope *(noun)* la speranza [spay-r*a*n-tzah]
  I hope that . . . spero che . . . [sp*a*y-roh kay]
  I hope so/not spero di sì/di no [. . . dee
  see/dee . . .]
horizon l'orizzonte [o-reet-tz*o*n-tay]
horn *(car)* il clacson
horrible orribile [or-*ree*-bee-lay]
hors d'oeuvre l'antipasto
horse il cavallo
hospital l'ospedale [os-pay-d*a*h-lay]
host(ess) l'ospite [*o*s-pee-tay]
  air hostess hostess

hot caldo
   (spiced) piccante [peek-kan-tay]
   it's too hot! scotta!
hotel l'albergo
» TRAVEL TIP: *hotels are divided into five
   categories: de luxe, first, second, third and
   fourth; hotel lists are issued by the provincial
   Tourist Board and by the local tourist offices
   (aziende autonome di soggiorno)*
hotplate il fornello
hot-water bottle la borsa dell'acqua calda
hour l'ora
house la casa [kah-sah]
   housewife la casalinga
how come [koh-may]
   how many? quanti [kwan-tee]
   how much? quanto? [kwan-toh]
   how often do the buses go? con che
   frequenza partono gli autobus? [kon kay
   fray-kwen-tzah par-toh-noh lee ow-toh-boos]
   how long does it take? quanto ci impiega?
   [. . . chee eem-pee-ay-gah]
   how long have you been here? da quanto
   tempo è qua? [. . . eh . . .]
   how are you? come sta? [koh-may stah]
hull lo scafo
humid umido [oo-mee-doh]
humour l'umorismo [oo-mo-rees-moh]
   haven't you got a sense of humour? non ha
   [ah] il senso dell'umorismo?
hundred cento [chen-toh]
hundredweight:
» TRAVEL TIP: *1 cwt = 50.8 kilos*
hungry: I'm hungry/not hungry ho fame/non
   ho fame [o fah-may . . .]
hurry: I'm in a hurry ho fretta [o frayt-tah]
   please hurry! per favore faccia presto!
   [. . . fa-voh-ray fah-chah pres-toh]
hurt: it hurts fa male [fah mah-lay]

my leg hurts mi fa mal la gamba [mee . . .]
YOU MAY THEN HEAR . . .
è un dolore acuto? [eh oon doh-*loh*-ray
a-*koo*-toh] *is it a sharp pain?*
husband: my husband mio marito [m*ee*-oh
ma-*ree*-toh]
I io [*ee*-oh]
I am sono
I leave tomorrow parto domani
ice il ghiaccio [ghee-*ah*-choh]
ice-cream il gelato [jay-l*ah*-toh]
iced coffee un caffè freddo [kaf-f*eh* . . .]
with lots of ice con molto ghiaccio
identity papers documenti di identità [. . . dee
ee-den-tee-t*ah*]
idiot idiota [ee-dee-*oh*-tah]
if se [say]
ignition l'accensione [a-chayn-see-*oh*-nay]
ill malato
I feel ill mi sento male [mee sen-toh m*ah*-lay]
illegal illegale [eel-lay-g*ah*-lay]
illegible illeggibile [eel-lay-j*ee*-bee-lay]
illness una malattia [ma-lat-*tee*-ah]
immediately immediatamente [–tay]
import importazione [–*oh*-nay]
important importante [–tay]
it's very important è molto importante
import duty dazio di importazione [d*ah*-tzee-oh
dee eem-por-ta-tzee-*oh*-nay]
impossible impossibile [eem-pos-s*ee*-bee-lay]
impressive imponente [–nayn-tay]
improve migliorare [meel-yo-r*ah*-ray]
I want to improve my . . . voglio migliorare il
mio . . . [v*ol*-yoh . . . m*ee*-oh]
in in [een]
he'll be here in a while sarà qua fra un po'
in London a Londra
in 1982 nel 1982 [nel
m*ee*l-lay-no-vay-chen-toh-ot-tan-ta-d*oo*-ay]

inch un pollice [pol-lee-chay]
» *TRAVEL TIP: 1 inch = 2.54 cm*
include includere [een-kloo-day-ray]
   does that include breakfast? è compresa la
   prima colazione? [eh kom-pray-sah lah
   pree-mah ko-la-tzee-*oh*-nay]
incompetent incompetente [–tay]
inconsiderate sconsiderato
incontinent incontinente [–tay]
incredible incredibile [–dee-bee-lay]
incrocio crossroads
indecent indecente [een-day-chen-tay]
independent indipendente [–tay]
India l'India [een-dee-ah]
   Indian indiano
indicator la freccia [fray-chah]
indigestion l'indigestione [–oh-nay]
indoors al coperto
industry industria [een-doos-tree-ah]
infection l'infezione [een-fay-tzee-oh-nay]
infectious contagioso [kon-ta-joh-soh]
inflation l'inflazione [een-fla-tzee-oh-nay]
informal senza formalità [sen-tzah
   for-ma-lee-tah]
**information: do you have any information in
   English about . . .?** ha delle informazioni in
   inglese su . . .? [ah del-lay een-for
   -ma-tzee-oh-nee een een-glay-say soo]
   is there an information office? c'è un ufficio
   di informazioni? [chay oon oof-fee-choh dee . . .]
ingresso entrance
   ingresso gratuito, ingresso libero admission
   free
inhabitant un abitante [–tay]
injection l'iniezione [een-yay-tzee-oh-nay]
injured ferito [fay-ree-toh]
   he's been injured è stato ferito [eh
   stah-toh . . .]
injury una lesione [lay-see-oh-nay]

innocent innocente [een-no-ch*e*n-tay]
insect un insetto
inside dentro
insist: I insist (on it) insisto [een-s*ee*s-toh]
insomnia l'insonnia
instant coffee il caffè istantaneo [kaf-f*e*h
   ees-tan-t*ah*-nay-oh]
instead invece [een-v*a*y-chay]
   instead of . . . invece di [. . . dee]
insulating tape il nastro isolante
   [. . . ee-so-l*a*n-tay]
insulation l'isolamento [ee-so-la-m*e*n-toh]
insult un insulto [een-s*oo*l-toh]
insurance l'assicurazione
   [as-see-koo-ra-tzee-*oh*-nay]
intelligent intelligente [–tay]
interesting interessante [–tay]
international internazionale
   [een-tayr-na-tzee-oh-n*ah*-lay]
interpret interpretare [–t*ah*-ray]
   would you interpret for us? può farci da
   interprete? [pwoh f*a*r-chee dah
   een-t*e*r-pray-tay]
into in [een]
introduce: can I introduce . . .? posso
   presentare . . .? [. . . pray-sayn-t*ah*-ray]
invalid *(noun)* un invalido [een-v*ah*-lee-doh]
   invalid chair una poltrona da invalido
invitation l'invito [een-v*ee*-toh]
   thank you for the invitation grazie
   dell'invito [gr*a*h-tzee-ay . . .]
» *TRAVEL TIP: when invited to an Italian house for a*
   meal it is customary to bring a cake or some ice
   cream, rather than wine
invite: can I invite you out? vuoi uscire con
   me? [vwoy oo-sh*ee*-ray kon may]
invoice la fattura
Ireland l'Irlanda
Irish irlandese [eer-lan-d*a*y-say]

iron *(clothes)* un ferro da stiro [. . . st*ee*-roh]
 will you iron these for me? mi può stirare
 questi? [mee pwoh stee-r*ah*-ray kw*es*-tee]
ironmonger's una ferramenta
is è [eh]
island l'isola [*ee*-so-lah]
it esso
 it's not working non funziona [non
 foon-tzee-*oh*-nah]
 is it . . .? è . . .? [eh]
 I'll take it lo prendo
Italian italiano
 an Italian woman un'italiana
 the Italians gli Italiani [lee . . .]
 I don't speak Italian non parlo l'italiano
Italy l'Italia [ee-t*a*l-yah]
itch il prurito [proo-*ree*-toh]
 it itches mi fa prurito [mee . . .]
itemize: would you itemize it for me? me lo
 dettaglia? [may lo dayt-t*a*l-yah]
IVA VAT
jack il cricco [kr*ee*k-koh]
jacket una giacca [j*a*k-kah]
jam la marmellata
 traffic jam un ingorgo
January gennaio [jen-n*ah*-yoh]
jaw la mascella [ma-sh*e*l-lah]
jealous geloso [jay-l*oh*-soh]
jeans i jeans
jellyfish una medusa
jetty il molo
jewellery i gioielli [jo-y*e*l-lee]
job un lavoro
 that's just the job va proprio a pennello
joke *(noun)* uno scherzo [sk*a*yr-tzoh]
 you must be joking sta scherzando
journey un viaggio [vee-*ah*-joh]
 have a good ,journey! buon viaggio!
 [bwon . . .]

July luglio [lool-yoh]
jumper un maglione [mal-yoh-nay]
junction un raccordo
June giugno [joon-yoh]
junk la robaccia [ro-bah-chah]
just: just two solo due [doo-ay]
  just a little solo un po'
  it's just there è lì [lee]
  not just now per ora no
  he was here just now era qua proprio ora
  that's just right è proprio giusto [eh
  pro-pree-oh joos-toh]
keen entusiasta [en-too-see-as-tah]
  I'm not keen non ne sono entusiasta
  [. . . nay . . .]
keep: can I keep it? lo posso tenere?
  [. . . tay-nay-ray]
  keep the change tenga il resto
  you didn't keep your promise non ha
  mantenuto la promessa [. . . ah . . .]
  it keeps on breaking si continua a rompere
  [see kon-tee-noo-ah ah rom-pay-ray]
kettle il bollitore [bol-lee-toh-ray]
» *TRAVEL TIP: electric kettles are not generally used*
  in Italy
key la chiave [kee-ah-vay]
kidney il rene [ray-nay]
  (meat) il rognone [ron-yoh-nay]
kill uccidere [oo-chee-day-ray]
kilo un chilo [kee-loh]
» *TRAVEL TIP: conversion:* $\dfrac{kilos}{5} \times 11 = pounds$

kilos	1	1½	5	6	7	8	9
pounds	2.2	3.3	11	13.2	15.4	17.6	19.8

kilometre un chilometro [kee-loh-may-troh]
» *TRAVEL TIP: conversion:* $\dfrac{kilometres}{8} \times 5 = miles$

kilometres	1	5	10	20	50	100
miles	0.62	3.11	6.2	12.4	31	62

kind: that's very kind of you è molto gentile da parte sua [eh . . . jen-*tee*-lay dah par-tay . . .]
kiss un bacio [b*a*h-choh]
kitchen la cucina [koo-c*h*ee-nah]
knee il ginocchio [jee-n*o*k-yoh]
knickers le mutande [moo-t*a*n-day]
knife il coltello [kol-t*e*l-loh]
knock bussare [boos-s*a*h-ray]
  there's a knocking noise from the engine il motore dà dei colpi [eel mo-t*o*h-ray dah day k*o*l-pee]
know sapere [sa-p*a*y-ray]
  (be acquainted with) conoscere [ko-n*o*h-shay-ray]
  I don't know non so
  I don't know the area non conosco queste parti [. . . kw*e*s-tay p*a*r-tee]
label l'etichetta [ay-tee-k*a*yt-tah]
laces *(shoes)* i lacci [l*a*h-chee]
lacquer la lacca
ladies *(toilet)* donne
» *TRAVEL TIP: only written: ask for* la toilette [twal*e*t]
lady una signora [seen-yo-rah]
lager una birra [b*ee*r-rah]
  lager and lime una birra col succo di cedro [. . . s*oo*k-koh dee ch*a*y-droh]
» *TRAVEL TIP: this is an unusual drink in Italy*
lake il lago [l*a*h-goh]
lamb l'agnello [an-y*e*l-loh]
lamp la lampada [l*a*m-pa-dah]
  lampshade il paralume [–*loo*-may]
  lamp-post il lampione [lam-pee-*oh*-nay]
land *(noun)* la terra
lane *(car)* la corsia [kor-s*ee*-ah]
language la lingua [l*ee*n-gwah]
large grande [gr*a*n-day]
laryngitis la laringite [la-reen-j*ee*-tay]
last ultimo [*oo*l-tee-moh]

last year/week l'anno scorso/la settimana scorsa

last night la notte scorsa [–tay]

at last! finalmente! [fee-nal-men-tay]

late: sorry I'm late scusi per il ritardo [skoo-zee . . .]

it's a bit late è un po' tardi [eh . . . tar-dee]

please hurry, I'm late in fretta per favore, sono in ritardo [. . . payr fa-voh-ray]

at the latest al più tardi [al pew . . .]

later più tardi

see you later a più tardi

latitude la latitudine [–too-dee-nay]

laugh (verb) ridere [ree-day-ray]

laundrette una lavanderia automatica [la-van-day-ree-ah ow-toh-mah-tee-kah]

» TRAVEL TIP: if you can't find a laundrette look for a 'lavasecco' (dry-cleaner's)

lavatory il gabinetto

lavori in corso men at work

law la legge [leh-jay]

lawyer l'avvocato

laxative un lassativo

lay-by l'area di parcheggio [ah-ray-ah dee par-kay-joh]

lazy pigro [pee-groh]

leaf la foglia [fol-yah]

leak: there's a leak in my ceiling il mio soffitto fa acqua [mee-oh sof-feet-toh . . .]

it leaks ha una perdita [ah oo-nah per-dee-tah]

learn: I want to learn . . . voglio imparare . . . [vol-yoh eem-pa-rah-ray]

lease (verb) affittare [–tah-ray]

least: not in the least proprio per niente [. . . nee-en-tay]

at least almeno [al-may-noh]

leather la pelle [pel-lay]

leather soles suole di cuoio [swo-lay dee kwo-yoh]

leave: we're leaving tomorrow partiamo
  domani
  when does the bus leave? quando parte
  l'autobus? [... par-tay low-toh-boos]
  I left two shirts in my room ho lasciato due
  camice in camera mia [o la-sh*ah*-toh d*oo*-ay
  ka-m*ee*-chay een k*ah*-may-rah m*ee*-ah]
  can I leave this here? posso lasciarlo qua?
left sinistra [see-n*ee*s-trah]
  on the left a sinistra
  left-handed mancino [man-ch*ee*-noh]
left luggage (office) il deposito bagagli
  [day-po-see-toh ba-g*al*-yee]
leg la gamba
legal legale [lay-g*ah*-lay]
lemon un limone [lee-m*oh*-nay]
lemonade una limonata [lee-mo-n*ah*-tah]
lend: will you lend me your ...? mi presta il
  suo ...? [mee ...]
lengthen allungare [al-loon-g*ah*-ray]
lens la lente [l*en*-tay]
Lent la Quaresima [kwa-r*ay*-see-mah]
less meno [m*ay*-noh]
  less than meno di [... dee]
  less than you think meno che non pensi
  [... kay ...]
let: let me help aspetti che l'aiuto [... kay
  la-y*oo*-toh]
  let me go! mi lasci andare! [mee l*ah*-shee
  an-d*ah*-ray]
  will you let me off here? mi fa scendere qua?
  [mee fah sh*en*-day-ray ...]
  let's go andiamo
  let me have a look mi faccia vedere [mee
  f*ah*-chah vay-d*ay*-ray]
letter la lettera [l*et*-tay-rah]
  are there any letters for me? ci sono lettere
  per me? [chee ... may]
  letterbox la cassetta delle lettere [... –ray]

lettuce l'insalata
level-crossing passaggio a livello [pas-s*ah*-joh ah lee-ve-loh]
liable *(responsible)* responsabile [res-pon-s*ah*-bee-lay]
libero vacant
library la biblioteca [bee-blee-o-t*ay*-kah]
licence il permesso
lid il coperchio [ko-per-kee-oh]
lie *(noun)* la menzogna [mayn-tzon-yah]
  can he lie down for a bit? può andare a riposarsi per un po'? [pwoh an-d*ah*-ray ...]
life la vita [*vee*-tah]
  life assurance l'assicurazione sulla vita [as-see-koo-ra-tzee-*oh*-nay sool-lah ...]
  lifebelt/life-jacket la cintura di salvataggio [cheen-*too*-rah dee sal-va-t*ah*-joh]
  lifeboat la scialuppa di salvataggio [sha-*loop*-pah dee ...]
  life-guard il bagnino [ban-*yee*-noh]
lift: do you want a lift? vuole un passaggio? [vw*oh*-lay oon pas-s*ah*-joh]
  could you give me a lift? mi può dare un passaggio? [mee pwoh d*ah*-ray ...]
  the lift isn't working l'ascensore non funziona [la-shayn-s*oh*-ray non foon-tzee-*oh*-nah]
light *(not heavy)* leggero [lay-j*ay*-roh]
  the lights aren't working la luce non funziona [la *loo*-chay non foon-tzee-*oh*-nah]
  (car) i fari non funzionano [ee f*ah*-ree non foon-tzee-*oh*-na-noh]
  have you got a light? ha da accendere? [ah da a-ch*en*-day-ray]
  when it gets light quando fa giorno [... j*or*-noh]
  light bulb la lampadina [–d*ee*-nah]
  light meter l'esposimetro [les-po-s*ee*-may-troh]

like: would you like . . .? vuole . . .? [vwoh-lay]
  I'd like a coffee vorrei un caffè [vor-ray oon kaf-feh]
  I'd like to go vorrei partire [. . .–tee-ray]
  I like you mi sei simpatico [mee say seem-pah-tee-koh]
  I like it/I don't like it mi piace/non mi piace [. . . mee pee-ah-chay]
  what's it like? com'è? [koh-meh]
  one like this uno come questo [. . . koh-may . . .]
  do it like this lo faccia così [lo fah-chah ko-see]
lime il cedro [chay-droh]
line la linea [lee-nay-ah]
lips le labbra
  lipstick il rossetto
  lip salve il burro di cacao [boor-roh dee ka-kah-oh]
liqueur un liquore [lee-kwoh-ray]
» TRAVEL TIP: **Sambuca:** *sort of anisette;* **amaro:** *bitter, made with herbs;* **Fernet:** *rather medicinal flavour, great for upset stomach or hangover;* **Strega:** *unique flavour, herb-based*
list *(noun)* la lista
listen ascoltare [–tah-ray]
litre un litro
» TRAVEL TIP: *1 litre = 1¾ pints = 0.22 gals*
little *(adjective)* piccolo
  a little ice/a little more un po' di ghiaccio/un po' di più [. . . dee ghee-ah-choh/. . . dee pew]
  just a little solo un po'
live vivere [vee-vay-ray]
  I live in Glasgow/in England abito a Glasgow/in Inghilterra [ah-bee-toh . . . een-gheel-ter-rah]
  where do you live? dove abita? [doh-vay ah-bee-tah]
liver il fegato [fay-ga-toh]
lizard la lucertola [loo-chayr-toh-lah]
loaf una pagnotta [pan-yot-tah]

lobster l'aragosta
local: could we try a local wine? possiamo
  provare un vino locale? [. . . pro-*vah*-ray oon
  vee-noh lo-*kah*-lay]
  a local restaurant un ristorante locale
  is it made locally? è fatto sul posto? [eh . . .]
lock la serratura
  the lock's broken la serratura è rotta
  I've locked myself out mi sono chiuso fuori
  [mee *soh*-noh kee-*oo*-soh fw*oh*-ree]
London Londra
lonely: are you lonely? ti senti solo? [tee . . .]
long lungo [*loon*-goh]
  we'd like to stay longer vorremmo stare più a
  lungo [. . . st*ah*-ray pew . . .]
  that was long ago questo era tanto tempo fa
  [. . . *eh*-rah]
longitude la longitudine [lon-jee-*too*-dee-nay]
loo: where's the loo? dov'è il gabinetto?
  [doh-v*eh* . . .]
look: you look tired mi sembra stanco
  [mee . . .]
  I'm looking forward to . . . non vedo l'ora
  di . . . [. . . v*ay*-doh . . . dee]
  I'm just looking sto guardando
  [. . . gwar-d*a*n-doh]
  I'm looking for . . . cerco . . . [ch*a*yr-koh]
  look at that guarda quello
  [gw*a*r-dah . . .]
  look out! attento!
loose allentato
  (clothes) largo
lorry l'autocarro [ow-toh-k*a*r-roh]
  lorry-driver il camionista
lose perdere [p*a*yr-day-ray]
  I've lost my . . . ho perso il mio . . . [o p*a*yr-soh
  eel m*ee*-oh]
  excuse me, I'm lost scusi, mi sono perso
  [sk*oo*-zee, mee . . .]

lost property (office) oggetti smarriti [o-jet-tee smar-*ree*-tee]

lot: a lot/not a lot molto/non molto
a lot of chips/wine tante patatine/tanto vino [*ta*n-tay pa-ta-*tee*-nay/*ta*n-toh *vee*-noh]
lots (of) un sacco (di) [. . . dee]
a lot more expensive molto più caro [. . . pew. . .]

lotion la lozione [lo-tzee-*oh*-nay]

loud: could you speak louder? può parlare più forte? [pwoh par-*lah*-ray pew *fo*r-tay]

love: I love you ti amo [tee *ah*-moh]
do you love me? mi ami? [mee *ah*-mee]
he's in love è innamorato [eh . . .]
I love this wine questo vino mi piace moltissimo [*kwes*-toh *vee*-noh mee pee-*ah*-chay . . .]

lovely bello

low basso

luck fortuna [for-*too*-nah]
good luck! buona fortuna! [bwo-nah . . .]

lucky fortunato [for-too-*nah*-toh]
you're lucky sei fortunato [say . . .]
that's lucky che fortuna [kay . . .]

luggage il bagaglio [ba-*ga*l-yoh]

lumbago la lombaggine [lom-b*ah*-jee-nay]

lump *(in the body)* un gonfiore [gon-fee-*oh*-ray]

lunch il pranzo [pr*a*n-tzoh]
(in Rome) la colazione [−tzee-*oh*-nay]

lung il polmone [pol-*mo*h-nay]

luxurious lussuoso

luxury il lusso [l*oo*s-soh]
a luxury hotel un albergo di [dee] lusso

mad matto

madam signora [seen-*yo*h-rah]

made-to-measure fatto su misura [. . . soo mee-*soo*-rah]

magazine una rivista [ree-v*ee*s-tah]

magnificent magnifico [man-*yee*-fee-koh]

maiden name il nome da signorina [noh-may dah seen-yo-ree-nah]

mail la posta; **is there any mail for me?** c'è posta per me? [cheh . . . may]

mainland il continente [—nen-tay]

main road la strada principale [. . . preen-chee-pah-lay]

make fare [fah-ray]

 will we make it in time? ce la faremo in tempo? [chay la fa-ray-moh . . .]

 make-up il trucco [trook-koh]

man un uomo [wo-moh]

manager il direttore [dee-ray-toh-ray]

 can I see the manager? posso parlare col direttore? [. . . par-lah-ray . . .]

manicure una manicure [ma-nee-koo-ray]

manners le maniere [man-yay-ray]

 haven't you got any manners? non ha un po' di educazione? [non ah oon po dee ay-doo-ka-tzee-oh-nay]

many molti [mol-tee]

map: a map of Italy una carta d'Italia **a map of Rome** una pianta di Roma [pee-an-tah dee . . .]

March marzo [mar-tzoh]

margarine la margarina [mar-ga-ree-nah]

marina il porto turistico [. . . too-rees-tee-koh]

mark: there's a mark on it c'è un segno [cheh oon sayn-yoh]

market place il mercato [mayr-kah-toh]

marmalade la marmellata d'arance [mar-mel-lah-tah da-ran-chay]

married sposato

marry: will you marry me? mi vuoi sposare? [mee vwoy-ee spo-sah-ray]

marvellous meraviglioso [may-ra-veel-yoh-soh]

mascara il mascara

mashed potatoes il purè di patate [poo-reh dee pa-tah-tay]

....

massage il massaggio [mas-*sah*-joh]
mast l'albero [al-*bay*-roh]
mat *(door)* lo stuoino [stwo-*ee*-noh]
(table) un sottopiatto
match un fiammifero [fee-am-m*ee*-fay-roh]
(short waxed match used by smokers) un cerino
[chay-*ree*-noh]
  a box of matches una scatola di fiammiferi
[sk*ah*-toh-lah dee . . .]
  football match una partita di calcio
[par-*tee*-tah dee k*a*l-choh]
material la stoffa
matter: it doesn't matter non importa
  what's the matter? cosa c'è? [. . . cheh]
mattress il materasso
mature maturo [ma-*too*-roh]
maximum massimo [m*a*s-see-moh]
May maggio [m*ah*-joh]
may: may I have . . .? potrei avere . . .? [po-tr*a*y
a-v*a*y-ray]
maybe forse [f*or*-say]
mayonnaise la maionese [mah-yo-n*a*y-say]
me: with me con me [kon may]
  he knows me mi conosce [mee ko-n*oh*-shay]
  it's me sono io [. . . *ee*-oh]
meal il pasto
mean: what does this mean? cosa vuol dire?
[. . . vwol d*ee*-ray]
  by all means! certamente! [chayr-ta-m*e*n-tay]
measles il morbillo
  German measles la rosolia [ro-so-l*ee*-ah]
measurements le misure [mee-*soo*-ray]
meat la carne [k*a*r-nay]
mechanic: is there a mechanic here? c'è un
meccanico qui? [cheh oon mayk-k*ah*-nee-koh
kwee]
medicine la medicina [may-dee-ch*ee*-na]
Mediterranean il Mediterraneo [−r*ah*-nay-oh]
meet: when shall we meet? a che ora ci

ritroviamo? [ah kay *oh*-rah chee . . .]
I met him in the street l'ho incontrato per
strada [lo . . .]; **pleased to meet you** piacere
[pee-ah-ch*ay*-ray]
meeting un incontro
melon un melone [may-l*oh*-nay]
member un socio [s*o*-choh]
   how do I become a member? come si diventa
soci? [k*oh*-may see dee-v*en*-tah s*o*-chee]
men gli uomini [lee w*o*-mee-nee]
mend: can you mend this? può aggiustare
questo? [pwoh a-joos-t*ah*-ray . . .]
mention: don't mention it prego [pr*ay*-goh]
menu il menù [may-n*oo*]
   can I have the menu, please? posso avere il
menù, per favore? [. . . a-v*ay*-ray . . . payr
fa-v*oh*-ray]
» *TRAVEL TIP: see pages 70–71*
mess: what a mess! che pasticcio! [kay
pas-t*ee*-choh]
   my room is in a mess la mia camera è in
disordine [lah m*ee*-ah k*ah*-may-rah eh een
dee-s*or*-dee-nay]
message: are there any messages for me? ci
sono messaggi per me? [chee s*oh*-noh
mays-s*ah*-jee payr may]
   can I leave a message for . . .? posso lasciare
un messaggio per . . .? [. . . la-sh*ah*-ray . . .]
metre un metro [m*ay*-troh]
» *TRAVEL TIP: 1 metre = 39.37 ins = 1.09 yds*
metropolitana underground
midday mezzogiorno [met-tzo-j*or*-noh]
middle mezzo [m*et*-tzoh]
   in the middle nel mezzo
midnight mezzanotte [met-tza-n*ot*-tay]
might: I might be late può darsi che faccia tardi
[pwoh d*ar*-see kay f*ah*-chah t*ar*-dee]
   he might have gone può darsi che se ne sia
andato [. . . kay say nay s*ee*-ah an-d*ah*-toh]

Antipasti: Starters
affettati misti *assorted cold meats*
prosciutto e melone *ham and melon*
insalata di frutti di mare *seafood salad*

Primi piatti: Soups and pasta
stracciatella *clear soup with eggs and cheese*
minestrone *thick vegetable soup*
zuppa di pesce *fish soup*
spaghetti alla carbonara *with egg and bacon
    sauce*
spaghetti al sugo *with meat sauce*
spaghetti al pomodoro *with tomato sauce*
lasagne al forno *layers of pasta and meat sauce
    covered with cheese and baked*
cannelloni *pasta stuffed with meat sauce and
    baked*
ravioli *pasta squares stuffed with meat or other
    savoury filling, served with a sauce*
gnocchi *potato dumplings*
risotto alla milanese *rice cooked in white wine
    and saffron with mushrooms and cheese*

Carni: Meat dishes
bistecca ai ferri/alla pizzaiola/alla
    fiorentina *grilled steak/steak with tomato
    sauce/grilled T-bone steak*
cotoletta alla milanese *veal cutlet in egg and
    breadcrumbs*
cotoletta d'agnello/di vitello *lamb/veal cutlet*
ossobuco *knuckle of veal in wine and tomato sauce*
saltimbocca alla romana *veal escalopes with ham
    and sage*
spezzatino di vitello *veal stew*

Pollame: Poultry
anitra all'arancio *duck in orange sauce*
pollo arrosto *roast chicken*
pollo alla cacciatora *chicken in a wine, onion and
    tomato sauce*

Pesce: Fish
baccalà *salt cod*
calamari in umido *squid in wine, garlic and tomato sauce*
fritto misto *mixed fried fish*
polipo ai ferri *grilled octopus*
sogliola al burro *sole in butter sauce*
trota ai ferri *grilled trout*

Contorni: Vegetables
patate: arrosto/fritte/cotte *potatoes: roast/fried/boiled*
puré di patate *mashed potatoes*
insalata mista *mixed salad*
pomodori al gratin *grilled tomatoes*
fagiolini al burro *French beans in butter*
finocchi al forno *fennel with cheese, browned in the oven*
melanzane al forno *baked aubergines in cheese sauce*
zucchini fritti *fried courgettes*

Formaggi: Cheese
Bel Paese *soft, full fat cheese*
caciotta *hard, medium fat cheese*
gorgonzola *soft, tangy blue cheese*
mozzarella *soft, sweet cheese made from buffalo's milk*
parmigiano *Parmesan*

Frutta e dolci: Desserts
macedonia *fruit salad*
bignè *profiteroles*
cassata *ice cream with candied fruit*
gelato *ice cream*
torta di mele/ciliege etc *apple/cherry etc tart*
zabaione *frothy dessert made with egg yolks, sugar and marsala wine*
zuppa inglese *trifle*

migraine l'emicrania [ay-mee-kran-yah]
mild *(weather)* mite [mee-tay]
  (cheese) dolce [dol-chay]
mile un miglio [meel-yoh]
» *TRAVEL TIP: conversion:* $\frac{miles}{5} \times 8 = kilometres$

miles	$\frac{1}{2}$	1	3	5	10	50	100
kilometres	0.8	1.6	4.8	8	16	80	160

milk il latte [lat-tay]
  a glass of milk un bicchiere di latte [oon beek-yeh-ray dee . . .]
  milkshake un frappé [frap-pay]
millimetre un millimetro [meel-lee-may-troh]
million un milione [meel-yo-nay]
milometer il contachilometri [–kee-lo-may-tree]
minced meat la carne tritata [kar-nay tree-tah-tah]
mind: I've changed my mind ho cambiato idea [o kam-bee-ah-toh ee-day-ah]
  I don't mind non importa
  I don't mind driving sono disposto a guidare [. . . gwee-dah-ray]
  do you mind if I . . .? le spiace se . . .? [lay spee-ah-chay say]
  never mind non fa niente [. . . nee-en-tay]
mine mio [mee-oh]
  that's mine questo è mio
mineral water l'acqua minerale [–rah-lay]
minimum minimo [mee-nee-moh]
minus meno [may-noh]
  it's minus 3 degrees ci sono tre gradi sotto zero [chee soh-noh tray grah-dee sot-toh tzay-roh]
minute minuto [mee-noo-toh]
  in a minute subito [soo-bee-toh]
  just a minute un momento
mirror lo specchio [spek-yoh]
Miss signorina [seen-yoh-ree-nah]

miss: I miss you mi manchi [mee-m*a*n-kee]
   Carlo's missing manca Carlo
   there's a . . . missing manca un . . .
mist la foschia [fos-k*ee*-ah]
mistake uno sbaglio [sb*a*l-yoh]
   I think you've made a mistake credo che si
   sia sbagliato [kr*a*y-doh kay see s*ee*-ah
   sbal-y*ah*-toh]
misunderstanding un malinteso [–t*a*y-soh]
modern moderno [–*a*yr-noh]
Monday lunedì [loo-nay-d*ee*]
money il denaro
   I've lost my money ho perso i soldi [o p*a*yr-soh
   ee s*o*l-dee]
   I've got no money sono senza soldi
   [. . . s*e*n-tzah . . .]
month un mese [m*a*y-say]
moon la luna [l*oo*-nah]
moorings gli ormeggi [lee or-m*a*y-jee]
moped il motorino [–r*ee*-noh]
more più [pew]
   can I have some more? posso averne ancora?
   [. . . a-v*a*yr-nay . . .]
   more wine, please ancora del vino per favore
   [. . . v*ee*-noh payr fa-v*oh*-ray]
   no more basta [b*a*s-tah]
   more comfortable più comodo
   more than più di [. . . dee]
morning il mattino [–t*ee*-noh]
   good morning buon giorno [bwon j*o*r-noh]
   this morning questa mattina
   in the morning di mattina [dee . . .]
   tomorrow morning domattina
mosquito una zanzara
most: I like it the most mi piace più di tutto
   [mee pee-*ah*-chay pew dee t*oo*t-toh]
   I like you the most mi piaci più di tutti
   [. . . pee-*ah*-chee . . .]
   most of the time la maggior parte del tempo

[ma-jor p*a*r-tay . . .]
most of the people il più della gente [d*e*l-lah
j*e*n-tay]
motel un motel
mother: my mother mia madre [m*ee*-ah
m*ah*-dray]
motor il motore [–ray]
motorbike la motocicletta [–chee-kl*a*yt-tah]
motorboat il motoscafo
motorcyclist il motociclista [–chee-kl*ee*s-tah]
motorist un automobilista
[ow-toh-mo-bee-l*ee*s-tah]
motorway l'autostrada [ow-toh-str*ah*-dah]
mountain la montagna [mon-t*a*n-yah]
mountaineer un alpinista
mountaineering l'alpinismo
mouse un topo
moustache i baffi [ee . . .]
mouth la bocca
move: don't move non si muova [non see
mw*o*-vah]
  could you move your car? può spostare la
  macchina? [pw*o*h spos-t*ah*-ray lah
  m*a*k-kee-nah]
Mr signor, Sig. [seen-y*o*r]
Mrs signora, Sig.ra [seen-y*o*-rah]
Ms *no equivalent*
much molto
  much better/much more molto meglio/molto
  di più [. . . m*e*l-yoh . . . dee pew]
  not much non molto
mug: I've been mugged sono stato assalito e
derubato [. . . st*ah*-toh as-sa-l*ee*-toh ay
day-roo-b*ah*-toh]
mum mamma
muscle il muscolo [m*oo*s-ko-loh]
museum il museo [moo-s*eh*-oh]
mushrooms i funghi [f*oo*n-ghee]
music la musica [m*oo*-see-kah]

must: I must have ... devo avere ... [d*a*y-voh
a-v*a*y-ray]
  I must not eat ... non devo mangiare ...
[man-j*a*h-ray]
  you must do it deve farlo [d*a*y-vay ...]
  must I ...? devo ...?
mustard la senape [s*a*y-na-pay]
my il mio [m*ee*-oh]; la mia; *(plural)* i miei [ee
mee-*eh*-ee]; le mie [–ay]
nail *(finger)* l'unghia [*oo*n-ghee-ah]
  (wood) il chiodo [kee-*o*-doh]
  nail clippers un tagliaunghie
[tal-yah-*oo*n-ghee-ay]
  nail file la limetta da unghie
[lee-m*a*yt-tah ...]
  nail polish lo smalto per unghie
  nail scissors le forbicine da unghie
[for-bee-ch*ee*-nay]
naked nudo [n*oo*-doh]
name il nome [n*oh*-may]
  my name is ... mi chiamo ... [mee
kee-*ah*-moh]
  what's your name? come si chiama?
[k*oh*-may see kee-*ah*-mah]
napkin il tovagliolo [toh-val-y*o*-loh]
nappy il pannolino [pan-no-l*ee*-noh]
narrow stretto
national nazionale [na-tzee-oh-n*ah*-lay]
  nationality la nazionalità [–tah]
natural naturale [na-too-r*ah*-lay]
naughty: don't be naughty non essere
impertinente [non *e*s-say-ray ... –tay]
near: is it near? è vicino? [eh vee-ch*ee*-noh]
  near here qui vicino [kwee ...]
  do you go near ...? va dalle parti di ...? [vah
d*a*l-lay p*a*r-tee dee]
  where's the nearest ...? dov'è il più
vicino ...? [doh-v*e*h il pew ...]
nearly quasi [kw*a*h-see]

neat *(drink)* liscio [*lee*-shoh]
necessary necessario [nay-chays-*sah*-ree-oh]
  it's not necessary non è necessario
neck il collo
  necklace la collana
need: I need a . . . ho bisogno di . . .
  [o bee-*sonn*-yoh dee]
needle un ago [*ah*-goh]
negotiations le trattative [lay trat-ta-*tee*-vay]
neighbour il vicino [vee-*chee*-noh]
neither: neither of them nessuno dei due
  [. . . day *doo*-ay]
  neither . . . nor . . . né . . . né . . . [nay . . .
  nay . . .]
  neither do I neanche io [nay-*an*-kay *ee*-oh]
nephew: my nephew mio nipote [*mee*-oh
  nee-*poh*-tay]
nervous nervoso
net la rete [*ray*-tay]
  net price prezzo netto [pret-tzoh]
never mai [*mah*-ee]
  well, I never! perbacco! [payr–]
  I never go there non ci vado mai [. . . chee
  v*ah*-doh . . .]
new nuovo [nw*o*-voh]
  New Year l'Anno Nuovo
  Happy New Year! Buon Anno! [bwon . . .]
  New Year's Eve la sera di Capodanno
  [. . . *say*-rah dee . . .]
  New Zealand la Nuova Zelanda
  [. . . tzay-l*an*-dah]
  New Zealander un neozelandese
  [nay-oh-tzay-lan-d*ay*-say]
news le notizie [no-*tee*-tzee-ay]
  newsagent il giornalaio [jor-na-l*ah*-yoh]
  newspaper il giornale [jor-n*ah*-lay]
  do you have any English newspapers? ha
  dei giornali inglesi? [ah day jor-n*ah*-lee
  een-gl*ay*-see]

next: the next day il giorno dopo [jor-noh . . .]
  sit next to me si sieda vicino a me [see
  see-*eh*-dah vee-ch*ee*-noh ah may]
  please stop at the next corner per favore si
  fermi al prossimo angolo [payr fa-v*oh*-ray see
  fer-mee al pr*o*s-see-moh *a*n-go-loh]
  see you next year arrivederci all'anno
  prossimo [ar-ree-vay-d*a*yr-chee . . .]
nice: a nice person una persona simpatica
  [. . . seem-p*a*h-tee-kah]
  a nice day una bella giornata
  [. . . jor-n*ah*-tah]
niece: my niece mia nipote [m*ee*-ah
  nee-p*oh*-tay]
night la notte [n*o*t-tay]
  good night buona notte [bw*o*-nah . . .]
  at night di notte [dee . . .]
  is there a good night club here? c'è un buon
  night club qua? [cheh oon bwon . . .]
  nightdress la camicia da notte
  [ka-m*ee*-chah . . .]
  night porter il portiere di notte
  [por-tee-*a*y-ray dee . . .]
nine nove [n*o*-vay]
  nineteen diciannove [dee-chan-n*o*-vay]
  nineteen eighty two/three
  millenovecentoottantadue/tré
  [m*ee*l-lay-no-vay-ch*e*n-toh-ot-tan-ta-d*o*o-ay/tr*a*y]
no no
  there's no water non c'è acqua [non cheh . . .]
  no way! certamente no!
  [chayr-ta-m*e*n-tay . . .]
  I've no money non ho denaro [. . . o . . .]
nobody nessuno
  nobody saw it non l'ha visto nessuno [non
  lah . . .]
noisy rumoroso
  our room's too noisy la nostra camera è
  troppo rumorosa [. . . k*ah*-may-rah eh . . .]

non toccare *do not touch*
none nessuno
   none of them nessuno di essi [. . . dee *es*-see]
nonsense sciocchezze [shok-k*ay*t-tzay]
normal normale [nor-m*ah*-lay]
north nord
   Northern Ireland l'Irlanda del Nord
nose il naso
   nosebleed il sangue al naso [s*an*-gway . . .]
not non
   I'm not hungry non ho fame [non o f*ah*-may]
   not that one non quello
   not me io no [*ee*-oh . . .]
   I don't smoke non fumo [non f*oo*-moh]
   I didn't order it non l'ho ordinato [non lo . . .]
note *(bank note)* una banconota
nothing niente [nee-*en*-tay]
November novembre [–bray]
now adesso
nowhere da nessuna parte [. . . p*ar*-tay]
nudist il nudista [noo-d*ees*-tah]
   nudist beach la spiaggia per nudisti
   [spee-*ah*-jah . . .]
nuisance: it's a nuisance! è una seccatura!
   [eh . . .]
   this man's being a nuisance quest'uomo sta
   dando fastidio [kwest-w*o*-moh . . .
   fas-*tee*-dee-oh]
numb intorpidito [een-tor-pee-d*ee*-toh]
number il numero [n*oo*-may-roh] *see page 128*
   number plate la targa
nurse l'infermiera [een-fer-mee-*ay*-rah]
nursery slope *(skiing)* la pista per principianti
   [p*ee*s-tah payr preen-cheep-y*an*-tee]
nut la noce [n*oh*-chay]
   (for bolt) il dado [d*ah*-doh]
oar il remo [r*ay*-moh]
obligatory obbligatorio [–t*oh*-ree-oh]
obviously ovviamente [–m*en*-tay]

occasionally a volte [vol-tay]
occupato *engaged*
occupied: is this seat occupied? è occupato?
[eh . . .]
o'clock *see* **time**
October ottobre [ot-toh-bray]
octopus il polipo [po-lee-poh]
odd *(number)* dispari [dees-pa-ree]
(strange) strano
of di [dee]
off: the milk/meat is off il latte è andato/la
carne è andata a male [eel lat-tay eh
an-dah-toh/la kar-nay eh an-dah-tah ah
mah-lay]
it just came off si è staccato [see . . .]
10% off uno sconto del dieci per cento
[. . . dee-ay-chee payr chen-toh]
offence un'offesa
office l'ufficio [oof-fee-choh]
official *(noun)* un ufficiale [oof-fee-chah-lay]
often spesso
oil l'olio [ol-yoh]
I'm losing oil perdo l'olio
will you change the oil? mi cambia l'olio?
[mee kam-bee-ah . . .]
ointment la pomata
OK okay
old vecchio [vek-yoh]
how old are you? quanti anni hai? [kwan-tee
an-nee ah-ee]
olive l'oliva [o-lee-vah]
olive oil l'olio d'oliva [ol-yoh . . .]
omelette la frittata
on su [soo]
I haven't got it on me non l'ho qui [non lo
kwee]
on Friday venerdì [–dee]
on television alla televisione
[. . . tay-lay-vee-see-oh-nay]

once una volta
  at once subito [soo-bee-toh]
one uno
  the red one quello rosso
onion una cipolla [chee-pol-lah]
only solo
  the only one l'unico [loo-nee-koh]
open *(adjective)* aperto
  I can't open it non riesco ad aprirlo [non
  ree-ays-koh . . .]
  when do you open? a che ora aprite? [ah kay
  oh-rah a-pree-tay]
opera l'opera [o-pay-rah]
operation l'operazione [o-pay-ra-tzee-oh-nay]
  will I need an operation? ho bisogno di una
  operazione? [o bee-sonn-yoh dee . . .]
operator *(phone)* il centralino
  [chen-tra-lee-noh]
» *TRAVEL TIP: for information dial 181*
opposite: opposite the hotel davanti
  all'albergo
optician l'ottico
or o
orange *(fruit)* l'arancia [a-ran-chah]
  (colour) arancione [a-ran-choh-nay]
  orange juice succo d'arancia [sook-koh . . .]
order: could we order now? possiamo
  ordinare adesso? [. . . or-dee-nah-ray . . .]
  thank you, we've already ordered grazie,
  abbiamo già ordinato [grah-tzee-ay
  ab-bee-ah-moh djah . . .]
other: the other one quell'altro
  do you have any others? ne ha degli altri?
  [nay ah day-lee al-tree]
otherwise altrimenti [–tee]
ought: I ought to go dovrei andare [doh-vray
  an-dah-ray]
ounce un'oncia [on-chah]
» *TRAVEL TIP: 1 ounce = 28.35 grammes*

our il nostro; la nostra
  that's ours è nostro
out: we're out of petrol siamo senza benzina
  [see-*ah*-moh sen-tzah ben-tz*ee*-nah]
  get out! fuori! [fw*oh*-ree]
outboard *(motor)* il fuoribordo
  [fwo-ree-bor-doh]
outdoors all'aperto
outside: can we sit outside? possiamo sederci
  fuori? [. . . say-d*ay*r-chee fw*oh*-ree]
over: over here/there qui/la [kwee/lah]
  he's over 40 ha più di quarant'anni [ah pew
  dee kwa-ran-t*a*n-nee]
  it's all over è tutto finito [eh . . .]
overboard: man overboard! uomo in mare!
  [wo-moh een m*ah*-ray]
overcharge: you've overcharged me mi ha
  fatto pagare troppo [mee ah f*at*-toh
  pa-*gah*-ray . . .]
overcooked troppo cotto
overexposed sovraesposto [so-vra-ays-pos-toh]
overnight *(stay)* per una notte [. . . n*ot*-tay]
  we've travelled overnight abbiamo
  viaggiato di notte [. . . vee-a-j*ah*-toh dee . . .]
oversleep: I overslept non mi sono svegliato
  [non mee s*oh*-noh svayl-y*ah*-toh]
overtake sorpassare [sor-pas-s*ah*-ray]
owe: what do I owe you? quanto le devo?
  [. . . lay d*ay*-voh]
own *(adjective)* proprio [pro-pree-oh]
  my own . . . il mio proprio . . . [m*ee*-oh . . .]
  I'm on my own sono da solo
owner il proprietario [pro-pree-ay-t*ah*-ree-oh]
oxygen l'ossigeno [os-s*ee*-jay-noh]
oysters le ostriche [os-tree-kay]
pack: I haven't packed yet non ho ancora fatto
  i bagagli [ee ba-g*al*-yee]
  can we have a packed lunch? potremmo
  avere un cestino da viaggio? [. . . a-v*ay*-ray oon

ches-*tee*-noh dah vee-*ah*-joh]
package tour il viaggio organizzato [vee-*ah*-joh
or-ga-neet-*tzah*-toh]
page *(of book)* la pagina [*pah*-jee-nah]
could you page him? può farlo cercare?
[pwoh *far*-loh chayr-*kah*-ray]
pain il dolore [doh-l*oh*-ray]
I've got a pain in my . . . ho [o] un dolore
al . . .
painkillers gli analgesici
[lee a-nal-j*ay*-see-chee]
painting un dipinto [dee-p*ee*n-toh]
pair un paio [p*ah*-yoh]
Pakistan il Pakistan
Pakistani pakistano
pale pallido [p*al*-lee-doh]
pancake la frittella
panties le mutandine [moo-tan-d*ee*-nay]
pants i pantaloni [ee . . .]
(underpants) le mutande [moo-t*a*n-day]
paper la carta
(newspaper) il giornale [jor-n*ah*-lay]
parcel il pacco
parcheggio parking
pardon *(didn't understand)* come? [k*oh*-may]
I beg your pardon *(sorry)* scusi [sk*oo*-zee]
parents: my parents i miei genitori
[ee mee-*eh*-ee jay-nee-t*oh*-ree]
park il parco
where can I park my car? dove posso
parcheggiare? [d*oh*-vay pos-soh
par-kay-j*ah*-ray]
part la parte [p*ar*-tay]
partenze departures
partner il compagno [kom-p*a*n-yoh]
party *(group)* la comitiva [ko-mee-*tee*-vah]
(celebration) la festa
I'm with the . . . party sono con la comitiva
di . . . [. . . dee]

pass *(mountain)* il passo
  he's passed out è svenuto [eh . . .]
passable *(road)* transitabile
  [tran-see-*tah*-bee-lay]
passaggio a livello level crossing
passenger il passeggero [pas-say-j*eh*-roh]
passer-by il passante [–tay]
passport il passaporto
past: in the past in passato
  see **time**
pastry la pasta
path il sentiero [sen-tee-*eh*-roh]
patient: be patient sia paziente [*see*-ah
  pa-tzee-en-tay]
pattern il disegno [dee-s*ayn*-yoh]
pavement il marciapiede [mar-cha-pee-*eh*-day]
pay pagare [pa-g*ah*-ray]
  can I pay, please? posso pagare, per favore?
  [. . . fa-v*oh*-ray]
peace la pace [p*ah*-chay]
peach una pesca
peanuts le arachidi [a-r*ah*-kee-dee]
pear una pera [p*ay*-rah]
peas i piselli [ee . . .]
pebble il ciottolo [ch*ot*-toh-loh]
pedal il pedale [pay-d*ah*-lay]
pedestrian il pedone [pay-d*oh*-nay]
  pedestrian crossing passaggio pedonale
  [pas-s*ah*-joh pay-doh-n*ah*-lay]
» *TRAVEL TIP: do not assume that cars will stop or
  even slow down for you at a pedestrian crossing*
pedoni pedestrians
peg *(clothes)* la molletta da bucato
  [. . . boo-k*ah*-toh]
  (tent) il picchetto [peek-k*ayt*-toh]
pelvis il bacino [ba-ch*ee*-noh]
pen la penna
  have you got a pen? ha una penna? [ah . . .]
pencil la matita [ma-t*ee*-tah]

penfriend il corrispondente [–tay]
penicillin la penicillina [pay-nee-cheel-*lee*-nah]
penknife il temperino [–*ree*-noh]
pensioner il pensionato
people la gente [*jen*-tay]
  the Italian people gli Italiani [lee . . .]
pepper il pepe [p*a*y-pay]
  (vegetable) il peperone [–nay]
peppermint la menta [m*a*yn-tah]
per per [payr]
  per person/night/week per persona/per
  notte/per settimana
per cent per cento [. . . ch*en*-toh]
perfect perfetto
  the perfect holiday la vacanza perfetta
  [va-k*a*n-tzah . . .]
perfume il profumo [pro-*foo*-moh]
perhaps forse [f*o*r-say]
pericolo danger
pericoloso sporgersi do not lean out
period il periodo [pay-*ree*-o-doh]
  (medical) le mestruazioni
  [mays-troo-a-tzee-*oh*-nee]
perm la permanente [–tay]
permit *(noun)* il permesso
person la persona
  in person in persona
petrol la benzina [ben-*tzee*-nah]
  petrol station il distributore di benzina
  [dees-tree-boo-t*oh*-ray dee . . .]
» *TRAVEL TIP:* '*normale*' = 2 star; '*super*' = 4 star
phone *see* **telephone**
photograph la fotografia [–*fee*-ah]
  would you take a photograph of us? ci fa la
  fotografia? [chee . . .]
piano il pianoforte [–tay]
pickpocket il borseggiatore [bor-say-ja-t*oh*-ray]
pie *(sweet)* la torta
  (savoury) il pasticcio [pas-*tee*-choh]

piece il pezzo [pet-tzoh]
  a piece of . . . un pezzo di . . . [. . . dee]
pig il maiale [ma-*yah*-lay]
pigeon il piccione [pee-ch*oh*-nay]
pile-up un incidente a catena [een-chee-d*e*n-tay
  ah . . .]
pill la pillola [p*ee*l-lo-lah]
  do you take the pill? prendi la pillola?
pillion: on the pillion sul sellino posteriore
  [sool sel-*lee*-noh pos-tay-ree-*oh*-ray]
pillow il cuscino [koo-sh*ee*-noh]
pin lo spillo [sp*ee*l-loh]
pineapple l'ananas
pink *(adjective)* rosa
pint la pinta [p*ee*n-tah]
» *TRAVEL TIP: 1 pint = 0.57 litres*
pipe il tubo [t*oo*-boh]
  (smoking) la pipa [p*ee*-pah]
  pipe tobacco il tabacco da pipa
piston il pistone [–nay]
pity: it's a pity è un peccato [eh . . .]
place il posto
  is this place taken? questo posto è occupato?
  do you know any good places to go? conosce
  dei posti interessanti? [ko-n*oh*-shay day pos-tee
  een-tay-rays-s*a*n-tee]
plain *(food)* semplice [s*e*m-plee-chay]
  (not patterned) senza nessun disegno [s*e*n-tzah
  nays-s*oo*n dee-s*a*yn-yoh]
plane l'aereo [ah-*eh*-ray-oh]
  by plane in aereo
plant la pianta [pee-*a*n-tah]
plaster *(medical)* il gesso [j*e*s-soh]
  see **sticking**
plastic la plastica [pl*a*s-tee-kah]
plate il piatto [pee-*a*t-toh]
platform *(rail)* il marciapiede
  [mar-cha-pee-*eh*-day]
  which platform, please? che binario, per

favore? [kay bee-*nah*-ree-oh payr fa-*voh*-ray]
play: somewhere for the children to play un
 posto dove i bambini possano giocare
 [. . . *doh*-vay ee bam-*bee*-nee pos-sa-noh
 jo-*kah*-ray]
pleasant piacevole [pee-a-ch*ay*-vo-lay]
please per favore [payr fa-*voh*-ray]
 could you please . . .? potrebbe . . .?
 [po-tr*ay*b-bay]
 yes, please sì, grazie [see gr*ah*-tzee-ay]
pleasure il piacere [pee-a-ch*ay*-ray]
 my pleasure prego [pr*ay*-goh]
plenty: plenty of . . . un sacco di . . . [. . . dee]
 thank you, that's plenty grazie, basta
 [gr*ah*-tzee-ay . . .]
pliers le pinze [p*ee*n-tzay]
plimsolls le scarpe di tela [lay sk*a*r-pay dee
 t*ay*-lah]
plug *(electrical)* la spina [sp*ee*-nah]
 (car) la candela [–d*ay*-lah]
 (bath) il tappo
» *TRAVEL TIP: you will need 2-pin plugs in Italy*
plum la prugna [pr*oo*n-yah]
plumber l'idraulico [ee-dr*ow*-lee-koh]
plus più [pew]
p.m. di pomeriggio [dee po-may-r*ee*-joh]
pneumonia la polmonite [pol-mo-n*ee*-tay]
poached egg un uovo affogato [wo-voh . . .]
pocket la tasca
point: could you point to it? me lo può
 indicare? [may lo pwoh een-dee-*kah*-ray]
 four point six quattro e sei [. . . ay say]
 points *(car)* le puntine [poon-*tee*-nay]
police la polizia [po-lee-tz*ee*-ah]
 get the police chiami la polizia
 [kee-*ah*-mee . . .]
 policeman il poliziotto [po-lee-tzee-*ot*-toh]
 police station il posto di [dee] polizia
» *TRAVEL TIP: most police duties are carried out by*

the Carabinieri; to contact the police dial 113
polish *(noun)* il lucido [loo-chee-doh]
  would you polish my shoes? potrebbe
  lucidarmi le scarpe? [po-tr*a*yb-bay
  loo-chee-d*a*r-mee lay sk*a*r-pay]
polite cortese [kor-t*a*y-say]
politics la politica [po-*lee*-tee-kah]
polluted inquinato [een-kwee-n*a*h-toh]
polythene bag un sacchetto di plastica
  [sak-k*a*yt-toh dee pl*a*s-tee-kah]
pool *(swimming)* la piscina [pee-sh*ee*-nah]
poor: I'm very poor sono molto povero
  [. . . po-vay-roh]
  poor quality di qualità scadente [dee
  kwa-lee-t*ah* ska-d*e*n-tay]
popular popolare [–ray]
population la popolazione
  [po-po-la-tzee-*oh*-nay]
pork il maiale [ma-y*a*h-lay]
port *(also drink)* il porto
  to port a babordo
porter il facchino [fak-k*ee*-noh]
portrait il ritratto
posh elegante [–tay]
possible possibile [pos-s*ee*-bee-lay]
  could you possibly . . .? potrebbe . . .?
  [po-tr*a*yb-bay]
post la posta
  post box la cassetta delle lettere [–ray]
  postcard la cartolina [kar-toh-*lee*-nah]
  post office l'ufficio postale [oof-*fee*-choh
  pos-t*ah*-lay]
» *TRAVEL TIP: postal service can be slow*
poste restante il fermo posta
potato la patata
pottery le terraglie [ter-r*a*l-yay]
pound *(sterling)* la lira sterlina [*lee*-rah
  ster-*lee*-nah]
  (weight) la libbra [*lee*b-brah]

» *TRAVEL TIP: conversion:* $\dfrac{pounds}{11} \times 5 = kilos$

pounds	1	3	5	6	7	8	9
kilos	0.45	1.4	2.3	2.7	3.2	3.6	4.1

pour: it's pouring sta piovendo a catinelle [stah pee-o-ven-doh ah ka-tee-nel-lay]

powder la polvere [pol-vay-ray]
 (face) la cipria [chee-pree-ah]

power cut: there's a power cut manca la corrente [–tay]

power point la presa (di corrente) [pray-sah dee kór-ren-tay]

prawns i gamberi [gam-bay-ree]
 prawn cocktail un cocktail di [dee] gamberi

prefer: I prefer this one preferisco questo

pregnant incinta [een-cheen-tah]

prescription la ricetta [ree-chet-tah]

present: at present adesso
 here's a present for you eccole un regalo [ek-ko-lay . . .]

president il presidente [. . . den-tay]

press: could you press these? mi può stirare questi? [mee pwoh stee-rah-ray kwes-tee]

pretty carino [ka-ree-noh]
 it's pretty expensive è assai caro [eh as-sah-ee . . .]

price il prezzo [pret-tzoh]

priest il prete [preh-tah]

printed matter stampe [stam-pay]

prison la prigione [pree-joh-nay]

private privato [pree-vah-toh]

probably probabilmente [–tay]

problem il problema

product il prodotto

profit il profitto

promise: do you promise? promette? [–tay]
 I promise prometto

pronounce: how do you pronounce

this? come si pronuncia? [k*o*h-may see pro-n*oo*n-chah]

pronto soccorso *first aid*

propeller l'elica [*eh*-lee-kah]

properly per bene [. . . b*a*y-nay]

prostitute una prostituta [pros-tee-t*oo*-tah]

protect proteggere [pro-t*eh*-jay-ray]

Protestant protestante [–t*a*n-tay]

proud orgoglioso [or-gol-y*oh*-soh]

prove: I can prove it posso provarlo

public: the public il pubblico [p*oo*b-blee-koh]

public convenience la toilette [twa-l*e*t]

» TRAVEL TIP: *not as many as in Britain, but most bars have a toilet that can be used free of charge*

public holidays i giorni festivi [j*o*r-nee fes-*tee*-vee]

» TRAVEL TIP: *public holidays: January 1st ('Capodanno'); Good Friday ('Venerdì Santo'); Easter Monday ('Pasqua'); April 25th; May 1st; August 15th ('l'Assunzione'); November 1st ('Ognissanti'); December 8th ('l'Immacolata Concezione'); December 25th ('Natale'); December 26th ('Santo Stefano')*

pudding il budino [boo-d*ee*-noh]

(dessert) il dolce [d*o*l-chay]

pull *(verb)* tirare [tee-r*ah*-ray]

he pulled out in front of me mi ha tagliato la strada [mee ah tal-y*ah*-toh la str*ah*-dah]

pump la pompa

punctual puntuale [poon-too-*ah*-lay]

puncture una foratura [fo-ra-t*oo*-rah]

pure puro [p*oo*-roh]

purple porpora [p*o*r-po-rah]

purse il borsello

push *(verb)* spingere [sp*ee*n-jay-ray]

pushchair il passeggino [pas-say-j*ee*-noh]

put: where can I put . . .? dove posso mettere . . .? [d*oh*-vay pos-soh m*e*t-tay-ray]

pyjamas il pigiama [pee-j*ah*-mah]

....

quality la qualità [kwa-lee-t*a*h]
quarantine la quarantena [kwa-ran-t*a*y-nah]
quarter un quarto [kw*a*r-toh]
 a quarter of an hour un quarto d'ora
 see **time**
quay il molo
question una domanda
queue *(noun)* la coda
» *TRAVEL TIP: the queueing habit is not very strong*
quick svelto
 that was quick è stato svelto [eh st*a*h-toh . . .]
quiet quieto [kwee-*a*y-toh]
 be quiet! zitto! [tz*ee*t-toh]
quite completamente [–tay]
 (fairly) assai [as-s*a*h-ee]
 quite a lot un sacco
race *(motor etc)* una corsa
radiator il radiatore [ra-dee-a-t*o*h-ray]
radio la radio [r*a*h-dee-oh]
rail: by rail col treno
rain la pioggia [pee-*o*-jah]
 it's raining piove [pee-*o*-vay]
 raincoat l'impermeabile
 [eem-per-may-*a*h-bee-lay]
rallentare **slow down**
rally *(car)* il rally
rape lo stupro [st*oo*-proh]
rare raro; *(steak)* al sangue [. . . s*a*n-gway]
raspberry il lampone [lam-p*o*h-nay]
rat un ratto
rather: I'd rather sit here preferisco sedere qui
 [. . . say-d*a*y-ray kwee]
 I'd rather not preferisco di [dee] no
 it's rather hot fa piuttosto caldo
 [. . . pewt-t*o*s-toh . . .]
raw crudo [kr*oo*-doh]
razor rasoio [ra-s*oh*-yoh]
 razor blades le lamette da barba
 [la-m*a*yt-tay . . .]

read: would you read it for me? me lo può leggere? [may loh pwoh l*e*h-jay-ray]
something to read qualcosa da leggere
ready: when will it be ready? per quando è pronto? [. . . eh . . .]
I'm not ready yet non sono ancora pronto
real autentico [ow-t*e*n-tee-koh]
real leather vera pelle [v*a*y-rah p*e*l-lay]
(shoes) vero cuoio [. . . kwo-yoh]
it's a real bargain è un vero affare [eh . . . af-f*a*h-ray]
really davvero [dav-f*a*h-roh]
rear-view mirror lo specchietto retrovisore [spayk-y*e*t-toh ray-tro-vee-s*o*h-ray]
reasonable ragionevole [ra-jo-n*a*y-vo-lay]
receipt la ricevuta [ree-chay-v*o*o-tah]
can I have a receipt, please posso avere la ricevuta, per favore? [pos-soh a-v*a*y-ray . . . payr fa-v*o*h-ray]
recently di recente [dee ray-ch*e*n-tay]
reception *(hotel)* il ricevimento [ree-chay vee-m*e*n-toh]
at reception al ricevimento
recipe la ricetta [ree-ch*e*t-tah]
recommend: can you recommend . . .? può consigliare . . .? [pwoh kon-seel-y*a*h-ray]
record *(music)* un disco [d*e*es-koh]
red rosso
reduction *(in price)* uno sconto
refuse: I refuse mi rifiuto [mee ree-f*e*w-toh]
region la regione [ray-j*o*h-nay]
registered letter una lettera raccomandata [l*e*t-tay-rah . . .]
regret: I regret that . . . mi rincresce che . . . [mee reen-kr*a*y-shay kay]
relax: I just want to relax voglio riposarmi [vol-yoh ree-po-s*a*r-mee]
remember: don't you remember? non si [see] ricorda?

I'll always remember mi ricorderò sempre [mee ree-kor-day-ro sem-pray]
something to remember you by qualcosa per ricordarti
rent: can I rent a car/boat/bicycle? posso affittare una macchina/barca/bicicletta? [... af-feet-tah-ray oo-nah mak-kee-nah/bar-kah/bee-chee-klayt-tah]
repair: can you repair it? può ripararlo? [pwoh ...]
repeat: could you repeat that? può ripetere? [pwoh ree-peh-tay-ray]
reputation la reputazione [ray-poo-ta-tzee-oh-nay]
rescue (verb) salvare [–ray]
reservation la prenotazione [pray-no-ta-tzee-oh-nay]
I want to make a reservation for ... vorrei fare una prenotazione per ... [vor-ray fah-ray ...]
reserve: can I reserve a seat? posso prenotare un posto? [... pray-no-tah-ray ...]
responsible responsabile [res-pon-sah-bee-lay]
rest: I've come here for a rest sono venuto qua per riposarmi
you keep the rest tenga il resto
restaurant il ristorante [–tay]
retail price il prezzo al minuto [pret-tzoh ...]
retired in pensione [een payn-see-oh-nay]
return: a return to ... un'andata e [ay] ritorno per ...
reverse gear la marcia indietro [mar-chah een-dee-eh-troh]
rheumatism il reumatismo [ray-oo-ma-tees-moh]
rib la costola [kos-toh-lah]
rice il riso [ree-soh]
rich ricco [reek-koh]
ridiculous ridicolo [ree-dee-ko-loh]

right: **that's right** è vero [eh-*vay*-roh]
    you're right ha ragione lei [ah-ra-j*oh*-nay lay]
    on the right a destra
    right now proprio adesso [pro-pree-oh . . .]
    (immediately) subito
    right here proprio qui [pro-pree-oh kwee]
    right hand drive la guida a destra [g*wee*-dah
    ah . . .]
ring *(on finger)* l'anello
ripe maturo [mat-*too*-roh]
rip-off: **it's a rip-off** è un furto [eh oon f*oo*r-toh]
riservato reserved
river il fiume [f*ew*-may]
road la strada
    which is the road to . . .? qual'è la strada
    per. . .? [kwa-l*eh* . . .]
    roadhog un guidatore incosciente
    [gwee-da-*toh*-ray een-ko-sh*e*n-tay]
rob: **I've been robbed** sono stato derubato
rock la roccia [ro-chah]
    whisky on the rocks un whisky con ghiaccio
    [ghee-*ah*-choh]
roll *(bread)* un panino [pa-*nee*-noh]
Roman Catholic cattolico [kat-*toh*-lee-koh]
romantic romantico [ro-m*a*n-tee-koh]
roof il tetto
room la camera [k*a*h-may-rah]
    have you got a (single/double) room? ha
    una camera (singola/doppia)? [ah . . .
    s*ee*n-go-lah/d*o*p-pee-ah]
    for one night/for three nights per una
    notte/per tre notti [. . . n*o*t-tay]
    YOU MAY THEN HEAR . . .
    con doccia *with shower*
    con bagno *with bath*
    spiacenti, ma siamo al completo *sorry, we're full*
room service il servizio [ser-*vee*-tzee-oh]
rope la fune [f*oo*-nay]
rose la rosa

rosé rosé
rough *(sea)* agitato
roughly *(approximately)* più o meno [pew o may-noh]
roulette la roulette
round *(circular)* rotondo
roundabout la rotonda
» *TRAVEL TIP: cars on the roundabout must give way to traffic joining the roundabout*
route: which is the prettiest/fastest route? qual'è la strada più bella/più veloce? [kwa-leh lah strah-dah pew bel-lah/pew vay-loh-chay]
rowing boat una barca a remi [. . . ray-mee]
rubber la gomma
  rubber band un elastico [ay-las-tee-koh]
rubbish una porcheria [por-kay-ree-ah]
  (garbage) la spazzatura [spat-tza-too-rah]
  rubbish! sciocchezze! [shok-ket-tzay]
rucksack lo zaino [tza-ee-noh]
rudder il timone [tee-moh-nay]
rude maleducato [ma-lay-doo-kah-toh]
ruins le rovine [ro-vee-nay]
rum il rum [room]
  rum and coke un rum e coca-cola [. . . ay . . .]
run: hurry, run! corri, fa presto!
  I've run out of petrol/money sono rimasto senza benzina/soldi [. . . sen-tzah ben-tzee-nah/sol-dee]
sad triste [trees-tay]
safe sicuro [see-koo-roh]
  will it be safe here? è al sicuro qua? [eh . . .]
  is it safe to swim here? è prudente nuotare qua? [–tay nwo-tah-ray . . .]
safety la sicurezza [see-koo-rayt-tzah]
  safety pin la spilla di sicurezza [speel-lah dee . . .]
sail le vela [vay-lah]
  can we go sailing? possiamo fare [fah-ray]

della barca a vela?
sailor il marinaio [ma-ree-n*ah*-yoh]
sala d'aspetto waiting room
salad l'insalata
» TRAVEL TIP: this refers only to vegetables: there is no such thing in Italy as a ham or cheese salad
salami il salame [–may]
saldi sale
sale: is it for sale? è in vendita [eh een v*a*yn-dee-tah]
salmon il salmone [sal-m*oh*-nay]
salt il sale [s*ah*-lay]
same stesso
the same again, please ancora dello stesso, per favore [. . . fa-v*oh*-ray]
the same to you altrettanto
sand la sabbia
sandal il sandalo [s*a*n-da-loh]
sandwich un panino imbottito [pa-n*ee*-noh eem-bot-*tee*-toh]
sanitary towels gli assorbenti igienici [lee . . . ee-j*a*y-nee-chee]
Sardinia la Sardegna [sar-d*a*yn-yah]
satisfactory soddisfacente [sod-dees-fa-ch*e*n-tay]
Saturday sabato [s*ah*-ba-toh]
sauce la salsa
saucepan la casseruola [kas-sayr-wo-lah]
saucer il piattino [pee-at-*tee*-noh]
sauna la sauna [s*ah*-oo-nah]
sausage la salsiccia [sal-s*ee*-chah]
save *(life)* salvare [sal-v*ah*-ray]
say: how do you say . . . in Italian? come si dice in italiano . . . ? [k*oh*-may see d*ee*-chay . . .]
what did he say? cosa ha detto? [. . . ha . . .]
scala mobile escalator
scarf il fazzoletto [fat-tzo-l*a*yt-toh]
scenery il panorama
schedule il programma

....

on/behind schedule in orario/in ritardo
scheduled flight il volo di linea [. . . dee
  lee-nay-ah]
school la scuola [skwo-lah]
scissors: a pair of scissors un paio di forbici
  [p*ah*-yoh dee for-bee-chee]
scooter il motorino [mo-to-*ree*-noh]
Scotland la Scozia [sko-tzee-ah]
Scottish scozzese [skot-tz*ay*-say]
scrambled eggs le uova strapazzate [lay wo-vah
  stra-pat-tz*ah*-tay]
scratch un graffio [gr*a*f-fee-oh]
scream un grido [gree-doh]
screw *(noun)* la vite [vee-tay]
  screwdriver il cacciavite [ka-cha-*vee*-tay]
sea il mare [m*ah*-ray]
  by the sea al mare
seafood i frutti di mare [ee fr*oo*t-tee dee
  m*ah*-ray]
search cercare [chayr-k*ah*-ray]
  search party squadra il soccorso [skw*ah*-drah
  dee . . .]
seasick: I get seasick soffro il mal di mare
  [. . . dee m*ah*-ray]
  I feel seasick ho il mal di mare [o . . .]
seaside la spiaggia [spee-*ah*-jah]
  let's go to the seaside andiamo al mare
  [. . . m*ah*-ray]
season la stagione [sta-j*oh*-nay]
  in the high/low season in alta/bassa stagione
seasoning il condimento
seat un posto a sedere [. . . say-d*ay*-ray]
  is this somebody's seat? è occupato questo
  posto?
  seat belt la cintura di sicurezza [cheen-*too*-rah
  dee see-koo-r*ay*t-tzah]
seaweed le alghe [*a*l-gay]
second secondo
  just a second un secondo

second hand di·seconda mano [dee . . .]
secret: it's a secret è un segreto [eh . . .]
see vedere [vay-*d*ay-ray]
   I see *(understand)* ho capito [o ka-*pee*-toh]
   have you seen . . .? ha visto . . .? [ah . . .]
   can I see the room? posso vedere la camera?
seem sembrare [saym-br*ah*-ray]
   it seems so pare di sì [p*ah*-ray dee see]
seldom raramente [ra-ra-m*e*n-tay]
self: self-service il self-service
   self-catering apartment un appartamento
   con l'uso cucina
sell vendere [v*a*yn-day-ray]
send spedire [spay-d*ee*-ray]
sensitive sensibile [sen-*see*-bee-lay]
sentimental sentimentale [−t*a*h-lay]
separate *(adjective)* separato [say-pa-r*ah*-toh]
   I'm separated sono diviso [. . . dee-*vee*-soh]
   can we pay separately? possiamo avere conti
   separati? [. . . a-v*a*y-ray . . .]
September settembre [−bray]
serious serio [*se*h-ree-oh]
   I'm serious sul serio
   this is serious questo è grave [. . . gr*ah*-vay]
   is it serious, doctor? è grave, dottore?
service: the service was excellent/poor il
   servizio era eccellente/lasciava a desiderare
   [ser-*vee*-tzee-oh *e*h-rah
   ay-chayl-l*e*n-tay/la-sh*ah*-vah ah
   day-see-day-r*ah*-ray]
service station la stazione di servizio
   [sta-tzee-*oh*-nay dee . . .]
serviette il tovagliolo [to-val-*yo*-loh]
several diversi [dee-*ve*r-see]
sexy sexy
shade: in the shade all'ombra
shake scuotere [skwo-tay-ray]
   to shake hands stringere la mano
   [str*ee*n-jay-ray lah m*ah*-noh]

» *TRAVEL TIP: customary to shake hands each time
you meet somebody and when you take your
leave of somebody*
shallow basso
shame: what a shame! che peccato! [kay . . .]
shampoo *(noun)* lo shampoo [sha m-poh]
  shampoo and set shampoo e messa in piega
  [. . . pee-*ay*-gah]
shandy birra e limonata [b eer-rah ay . . .]
» *TRAVEL TIP: beer is lager-type*
share *(room, table)* dividere [dee-v ee-day-ray]
shark lo squalo [skw ah-loh]
sharp *(pain)* acuto [a-koo-toh]
  (blade) affilato
  (taste) acido [ah-chee-doh]
  (bend) stretto
shave radersi [r ah-dayr-see]
  shaver un rasoio [ra-s oh-yoh]
  shaving point la presa per il rasoio
  shaving foam schiuma da barba
  [sk ew-mah . . .]
she lei [lay]
  she is è [eh]
sheep la pecora [p eh-ko-rah]
sheet il lenzuolo [len-tzwo-loh]
shelf lo scaffale [skaf-f ah-lay]
shell la conchiglia [kon-k eel-yah]
  shellfish i molluschi [ee mol-l oos-kee]
shelter *(noun)* un riparo
  can we shelter here? possiamo ripararci qua?
  [. . . ree-pa-r ar-chee . . .]
sherry lo sherry
shin la tibia [t ee-bee-ah]
ship la nave [n ah-vay]
  by ship con la nave
shirt la camicia [ka-m ee-chah]
shock *(noun: surprise)* lo shock
  I got an electric shock from the . . . ho preso
  la scossa con . . . [o . . .]

....

shock-absorber l'ammortizzatore
[am-mor-teet-tza-*toh*-ray]
shoe la scarpa
» *TRAVEL TIP: shoe sizes*
UK	4	5	6	7	8	9	10	11
Italy	37	38	39	41	42	43	44	46

shop il negozio [nay-go-tzee-oh]
I've some shopping to do devo fare delle
compere [*day*-voh f*ah*-ray d*e*l-lay kom-pay-ray]
» *TRAVEL TIP: shops usually close for lunch*
between 12.30 and 3.30 in winter, 12.30 and 4.30
in summer, and remain open till 7 or 8 p.m.
shore la costa
on the shore sulla spiaggia [s*oo*l-lah
spee-*ah*-jah]
short corto
I'm three short me ne mancano tre [may nay
m*a*n-ka-noh tray]
short cut la scorciatoia [skor-cha-*toh*-yah]
shorts i calzoncini [ee kal-tzon-ch*ee*-nee]
shoulder la spalla
shout *(verb)* gridare [gree-d*ah*-ray]
show: please show me mi può mostrare? [mee
pwoh mos-tr*ah*-ray]
shower: with shower con doccia [d*oh*-chah]
shrimps i gamberetti
shrink: it's shrunk si è ristretto [see . . .]
shut *(verb)* chiudere [kee-*oo*-day-ray]
when do you shut? a che ora chiudete? [ah
kay *oh*-rah kee-oo-d*ay*-tay]
shut up! sta'zitto! [stah-tz*ee*t-toh]
shy timido [*tee*-mee-doh]
si prega di non . . . please do not . . .
Sicily la Sicilia [see-ch*ee*l-yah]
sick malato [ma-l*ah*-toh]
I feel sick mi sento male [mee s*e*n-toh
m*ah*-lay]
he's been sick è stato male [eh st*ah*-toh . . .]
side il lato [l*ah*-toh]

side light la luce di posizione [loo-chay dee po-see-tzee-*oh*-nay]
side street una laterale [–lay]
by the side of the road sul margine della strada [sool m*a*r-jee-nay . . .]
sight: out of sight fuori vista [fw*oh*-ree v*ee*s-tah]
we'd like to go on a sightseeing tour vorremmo fare una gita turistica [. . . f*a*h-ray oo-nah j*ee*-tah too-r*ee*s-tee-kah]
sign *(notice)* il cartello
signal: he didn't signal non ha indicato [non ah een-dee-k*a*h-toh]
signature la firma
signore *ladies*
signori *gentlemen*
silence *(noun)* il silenzio [see-l*e*n-tzee-oh]
silencer il silenziatore [see-len-tzee-a-t*oh*-ray]
silk la seta [s*a*y-tah]
silly sciocco [sh*o*k-koh]
silver l'argento [ar-j*e*n-toh]
similar simile [s*ee*-mee-lay]
simple semplice [s*a*ym-plee-chay]
since: since last week dalla settimana scorsa
since we arrived da quando siamo arrivati
(because) poiché [poy-k*a*y]
sincere sincero [seen-ch*a*y-roh]
yours sincerely cordiali saluti
sing cantare [kan-t*a*h-ray]
single: single room una camera singola [k*a*h-may-rah s*ee*n-go-lah]
I'm single non sono sposato
a single to . . . un'andata per . . . [oon an-d*a*h-tah . . .]
sink: it sank è affondato
sir signore [seen-y*oh*-ray]
sister: my sister mia sorella [m*ee*-ah . . .]
sit: can I sit here? posso sedermi qui? [. . . say-d*a*yr-mee kwee]

size *(clothes)* la taglia [tal-yah]
  (shoes) il numero [noo-may-roh]
ski *(noun)* lo sci [shee]
  (verb) sciare [shee-*ah*-ray]
  skiing lo sciare
  ski boots gli scarponi da sci [lee skar-p*oh*-nee dah shee]
  ski lift la sciovia [shee-o-v*ee*-ah]
  ski pants i pantaloni da sci [pan-ta-l*oh*-nee . . .]
  ski pole la racchetta da sci [rak-k*ay*t-tah . . .]
  ski slope/ski run la pista da sci [p*ee*s-tah . . .]
  ski wax la sciolina [shee-o-l*ee*-nah]
skid sbandare [sban-d*ah*-ray]
skin la pelle [pel-lay]
  skin diving il nuoto subacqueo [nwo-toh soo-b*ah*-kway-oh]
» *TRAVEL TIP: see* **aqualung**
skirt la gonna
sky il cielo [ch*ay*-loh]
  in the sky in cielo
sledge la slitta
sleep: **I can't sleep** non riesco a dormire [. . . ree-*ay*s-koh ah dor-m*ee*-ray]
  sleeper *(rail)* il vagone letto [va-g*oh*-nay . . .]
  sleeping bag il sacco a pelo
  sleeping pill un sonnifero [sonn-n*ee*-fay-roh]
  YOU MAY HEAR . . .
  ha dormito bene? *did you sleep well?*
sleeve la manica [m*ah*-nee-kah]
slide *(photo)* una diapositiva [dee-a-po-see-t*ee*-vah]
slow: **could you speak a little slower?** può parlare un po' più lentamente? [pwoh par-l*ah*-ray oon po pew len-ta-m*ay*n-tay]
small piccolo
  small change la moneta [mo-n*ay*-tah]
smell: **there's a funny smell** c'è un odore strano [chay oon o-d*oh*-ray . . .]

....

 it smells puzza [poot-tzah]
smile *(verb)* sorridere [sor-ree-day-ray]
smoke *(noun)* il fumo [foo-moh]
 do you smoke? fuma?
 can I smoke? posso fumare? [. . . foo-mah-ray]
smooth liscio [lee-shoh]
snack spuntino [spoon-tee-noh]
 can we just have a snack? non vorremmo un
 pasto completo
snake una serpe [–pay]
snorkel un respiratore [–toh-ray]
snow *(noun)* la neve [nay-vay]
so: it's so hot fa così caldo [. . . ko-see . . .]
 not so much non così tanto
 so-so così-così
soap il sapone [sa-poh-nay]
 soap powder il detersivo [day-tayr-see-voh]
sober non ubriaco [. . . oo-bree-ah-koh]
socks i calzini [kal-tzee-nee]
soda (water) l'acqua di [dee] soda
soft drink un analcolico [a-nal-ko-lee-koh]
sole *(shoe)* la suola [swoh-lah]
 could you put new soles on these? può
 risuolarmi queste? [pwoh ree-swo-lar-mee
 kwes-tay]
 YOU MAY THEN HEAR . . .
 di cuoio o di gomma? *leather or rubber?*
some: some people alcune persone [al-koo-nay
 per-soh-nay]
 can I have some? posso averne un po'?
 [. . . a-vayr-nay . . .]
 can I have some grapes/some bread? posso
 avere dell'uva/del pane? [. . . a-vay-ray
 del-loo-vah/del pah-nay]
 can I have some more? posso averne ancora
 [. . . a-vayr-nay . . .]
 that was some meal! però che pranzo [pay-ro
 kay pran-tzoh]
 somebody qualcuno [kwal-koo-noh]

something qualcosa
sometimes a volte [ah vol-tay]
somewhere da qualche parte [. . . kwal-kay par-tay]
son: my son mio figlio [mee-oh feel-yoh]
song una canzone [kan-tzoh-nay]
soon presto
  as soon as possible appena possibile [. . . pos-see-bee-lay]
  sooner prima [pree-mah]
sore: it's sore mi fa male [mee fah mah-lay]
  sore throat il mal di gola [. . . dee . . .]
sorry: (I'm) sorry mi spiace [mee spee-ah-chay]
sort: this sort questo tipo [. . . tee-poh]
  what sort of . . .? che tipo di . . .? [kay tee-poh dee]
  will you sort it out? ci pensa lei? [chee pen-sah lay]
sosta autorizzata (9–12) parking (between 9 and 12)
sosta vietata no waiting
sottopassaggio underpass
soup la zuppa [tzoop-pah]
south sud [sood]
South Africa il Sudafrica [soo-dah-free-kah]
South African sudafricano
souvenir un souvenir
spade la vanga
  (child's) la paletta
spaghetti gli spaghetti [lee spa-gayt-tee]
spanner la chiave inglese [kee-ah-vay een-glay-say]
spare: spare part il pezzo di ricambio [pet-tzoh dee ree-kam-bee-oh]
  spare wheel la ruota di scorta [rwo-tah dee . . .]
spark(ing) plug la candela
speak: do you speak English? parla l'inglese? [. . . leen-glay-say]

I don't speak Italian non parlo l'italiano
special speciale [spay-ch*ah*-lay]
specialist lo specialista [spay-cha-l*ees*-tah]
specially specialmente [spay-chal-m*ay*n-tay]
spectacles gli occhiali da vista [lee
  ok-y*ah*-lee . . .]
speed la velocità [vay-lo-chee-t*ah*]
  he was speeding aveva superato il limite di
  velocità [. . . l*ee*-mee-tay dee . . .]
  speed limit il limite di velocità
  speedometer il tachimetro [ta-k*ee*-may-troh]
spend *(money)* spendere [sp*e*n-day-ray]
spices le spezie [sp*e*t-zee-ay]
  is it spicy? è piccante? [eh peek-k*a*n-tay]
  it's too spicy è troppo piccante
spider il ragno [r*a*n-yoh]
spingere push
spirits le bevande alcoliche [lay bay-v*a*n-day
  al-k*o*-lee-kay]
spoon il cucchiaio [kook-y*ah*-yoh]
sprain *(noun)* una storta
  I've sprained my ankle ho preso una storta
  alla caviglia [o . . . ka v*ee*l-yah]
spring la molla
  (season) la primavera [pree-ma-v*eh*-rah]
square *(in town)* la piazza [pee-*a*t-tzah]
  two square metres due metri quadri
  [d*oo*-ay . . .]
stairs le scale [lay sk*ah*-lay]
stall: it keeps stalling non fa altro che fermarsi
  [. . . kay . . .]
stalls *(theatre)* la platea [pla-t*eh*-ah]
stamp il francobollo [fran-ko-b*o*l-loh]
  two stamps for Britain, please due
  francobolli per l'Inghilterra, per favore
  [d*oo*-ay . . . payr leen-gheel-t*e*r-rah, payr
  fa-v*oh*-ray]
  » *TRAVEL TIP: buy stamps at tobacconists and most*
  bars

stand *(verb)* stare in piedi [st*ah*-ray een pee-*eh*-dee]
  (at fair) lo stand
standard *(adjective)* medio [m*e*d-yoh]
  standard model un modello standard
stand-by di riserva [dee . . .]
star una stella
starboard tribordo [tree-b*o*r-doh]
start: my car won't start la macchina non parte [m*a*k-kee-nah non p*a*r-tay]
  when does it start? quando comincia? [kw*a*n-doh ko-m*ee*n-chah]
starter *(car)* il motorino d'avviamento [mo-to-r*ee*-noh dav-vee-a-m*a*yn-toh]
starving: I'm starving sto morendo di fame [. . . dee f*ah*-may]
station la stazione [sta-tzee-*oh*-nay]
statue la statua [st*ah*-too-ah]
stay: we enjoyed our stay abbiamo avuto un soggiorno piacevole [ab-bee-*ah*-moh a-v*oo*-toh oon so-j*o*r-noh pee-a-ch*a*y-vo-lay]
  stay there resta lì [. . . lee]
  I'm staying at . . . sono al . . .
steak la bistecca [bees-t*a*yk-kah]
  YOU MAY HEAR . . .
  al sangue [al s*a*n-gway] *rare*
  poco cotta *medium rare*
  cotta bene [. . . b*a*y-nay] *well done*
steep ripido [r*ee*-pee-doh]
steering *(car)* lo sterzo [st*a*yr-tzoh]
  steering wheel il volante [–tay]
step *(stairs)* il gradino [gra-d*ee*-noh]
stereo stereo
sterling *(pound)* la sterlina [stayr-l*ee*-nah]
stewardess la hostess
sticking plaster il cerotto [chay-r*o*t-toh]
sticky appiccicoso [ap-pee-chee-k*oh*-soh]
stiff rigido [r*ee*-jee-doh]
still *(adjective)* calmo [k*a*l-mo]

keep still sta' fermo
I'm still here sono ancora qui
stink *(noun)* una puzza [p*oo*t-tzah]
stolen: my wallet's been stolen mi hanno rubato il portafoglio [mee-*a*n-noh roo-b*ah*-toh eel por-ta-f*o*l-yoh]
stomach lo stomaco [st*o*-ma-koh]
   I've got stomach-ache ho il mal di stomaco [o eel mal dee . . .]
   have you got something for an upset stomach? ha qualcosa per il mal di stomaco? [ah . . .]
stone la pietra [pee-eh-trah]
» *TRAVEL TIP: 1 stone = 6.35 kilos*
stop: stop! ferma!
   stop-over la fermata
   do you stop near . . .? si ferma vicino . . .? [see f*e*r-mah vee-ch*ee*-noh ah]
storm il temporale [taym-po-r*ah*-lay]
straight diritto [dee-r*ee*t-toh]
   go straight on sempre diritto [sem-pray . . .]
   straight away subito [s*oo*-bee-toh]
   straight whisky un whisky liscio [l*ee*-shoh]
strange strano
stranger un estraneo [es-trah-nay-oh]
   I'm a stranger here non sono pratico del luogo [. . . pr*a*h-tee-koh del lwo-goh]
strawberry la fragola [fr*a*h-go-lah]
street la strada
string: have you got any string? ha della corda? [ah . . .]
striptease lo striptease
stroke: he's had a stroke gli è venuto un attacco [lee eh vay-n*oo*-toh . . .]
strong forte [f*o*r-tay]
student uno studente [stoo-d*e*n-tay]
stung: I've been stung sono stato punto [. . . p*oo*n-toh]
stupid stupido [st*oo*-pee-doh]

such: such a lot così tanto [ko-*see* . . .]
suddenly improvvisamente [–tay]
sugar lo zucchero [tz*oo*-kay-roh]
suit *(man's)* l'abito [*ah*-bee-toh]
   (woman's) il tailleur [ta-yoor]
   suitcase una valigia [va-*lee*-jah]
suitable adatto
summer l'estate [es-*tah*-tay]
sun il sole [s*oh*-lay]
   in the sun al sole
   out of the sun all'ombra
   sunbathe prendere il sole [pren-day-ray . . .]
   sunburn la scottatura [skot-ta-*too*-rah]
   sunglasses gli occhiali da sole [lee
   ok-*yah*-lee . . .]
   suntan oil l'olio solare [l*ol*-yoh so-*lah*-ray]
   sunstroke il colpo di [dee] sole
Sunday domenica [doh-m*ay*-nee-kah]
suonare *please ring*
supermarket il supermercato
supper la cena [ch*ay*-nah]
sure: I'm not sure non sono sicuro [see-k*oo*-roh]
   sure! certamente! [chayr-ta-m*ay*n-tay]
   are you sure? è sicuro? [eh . . .]
surfboard la tavola da surfing
surfing: to go surfing andare a fare il surfing
   [an-d*ah*-ray ah f*ah*-ray eel . . .]
surname il cognome [kon-y*oh*-may]
swear word una parolaccia [pa-ro-*lah*-chah]
sweat *(verb)* sudare [soo-d*ah*-ray]
sweet: it's too sweet è troppo dolce [eh . . .
   d*ol*-chay]
   (dessert) il dolce
sweets caramelle [–lay]
swerve: I had to swerve ho dovuto deviare
   improvvisamente [o do-*voo*-toh day-vee-*ah*-ray
   eem-prov-vee-sa-m*en*-tay]
swim: I'm going for a swim vado a fare una
   nuotata [v*ah*-doh ah f*ah*-ray *oo*-nah

nwo-t*ah*-tah]
swimming costume il costume da bagno
[kos-*too*-may dah b*a*n-yoh]
  swimming pool la piscina [pee-sh*ee*-nah]
Swiss svizzero [sv*ee*t-tzay-roh]
Switzerland la Svizzera [sv*ee*t-tzay-rah]
switch *(noun)* l'interruttore
[een-ter-root-t*oh*-ray]
  to switch (something)
  on/off accendere/spegnere (qualcosa)
[a-ch*e*n-day-ray/sp*e*n-yay-ray . . .]
table la tavola [t*ah*-vo-lah]
  a table for 4 un tavolo per quattro
  table wine un vino da pasto [v*ee*-noh . . .]
take prendere [pr*e*n-day-ray]
  can I take this with me? posso prendere
  questo?
  will you take me to the airport? mi può
  condurre all'aeroporto? [mee pwoh
  kon-d*oo*r-ray al-la-ay-ro-p*o*r-toh]
  how long will it take? quanto ci vorrà?
  [. . . chee . . .]
  somebody has taken my bags qualcuno ha
  preso le mie valigie [. . . ah pr*a*y-soh lay m*ee*-ay
  va-l*ee*-jay]
  can I take you out tonight? posso portarti
  fuori questa sera? [. . . fw*oh*-ree . . .]
  is this seat taken? è occupato? [eh . . .]
talcum powder il borotalco
talk *(verb)* parlare [par-l*ah*-ray]
tall alto
tampons i tamponi [ee tam-p*oh*-nee]
tan l'abbronzatura [ab-bron-tza-*too*-rah]
  I want to get a tan voglio abbronzarmi
  [v*o*l-yoh ab-bron-tz*a*r-mee]
tank *(of car)* il serbatoio [sayr-ba-t*oh*-yoh]
tap il rubinetto [roo-bee-n*a*yt-toh]
tape il nastro
tape recorder il registratore

[ray-jees-tra-*toh*-ray]

tariff la tariffa

taste *(noun) (food)* il sapore [sa-p*oh*-ray]
(clothes etc) il gusto [g*oos*-toh]
  can I taste it? posso assaggiare?
  [as-sa-j*ah*-ray]
  it tastes horrible/very nice fa schifo/è molto
  buono [fah sk*ee*-foh/eh m*o*l-toh bw*o*-noh]

taxi il tassì [tas-*see*]
  will you get me a taxi? mi può chiamare un
  tassì? [mee pwoh kee-a-m*ah*-ray . . .]
  where can I get a taxi? dove posso prendere
  un tassì? [d*oh*-vay p*o*s-soh pr*e*n-day-ray . . .]
  taxi-driver il tassista

tea il tè [teh]
  could I have some tea? posso avere un tè?
  [. . . a-v*ay*-ray . . .]
  tea with milk/with lemon tè al latte/al
  limone [. . . l*a*t-tay/al lee-m*oh*-nay]
  teapot una teiera [tay-yeh-rah]
  » *TRAVEL TIP: tea is usually served either black or*
  with lemon ('al limone'); tea with milk is very
  unusual and milk must be ordered separately

teach: could you teach me? mi può insegnare?
  [mee pwoh een-sayn-y*ah*-ray]

teacher l'insegnante [een-sayn-y*a*n-tay]

telegram il telegramma
  I want to send a telegram vorrei spedire un
  telegramma [vor-r*a*y spay-d*ee*-ray . . .]

telephone *(noun)* il telefono [tay-*leh*-fo-noh]
  can I make a phone-call? posso fare una
  telefonata? [. . . f*ah*-ray . . .]
  can I speak to . . .? posso parlare con . . .?
  [. . . par-*lah*-ray . . .]
  could you get this number for me? mi può
  chiamare questo numero? [mee pwoh
  kee-ah-m*ah*-ray kw*e*s-toh n*oo*-may-roh]
  telephone directory l'elenco telefonico
  [. . . tay-lay-fo-nee-koh]

....

» *TRAVEL TIP: for public phones you'll need tokens*
  (gettoni), 1 for local, min. of 6 for international
  calls; buy gettoni at tobacconists, bars, post
  offices, newsagents; code for UK is 0044 and
  drop first 0 of UK area code; in larger towns go to
  SIP where the assistant will put you through
television la televisione
  [tay-lay-vee-see-*oh*-nay]
  I'd like to watch television vorrei guardare
  la televisione
  [vor-r*ay* gwar-d*ah*-ray . . .]
tell: could you tell me where . . .? mi può dire
  dove . . .? [mee pwoh d*ee*-ray d*oh*-vay]
temperature *(weather etc)* la temperatura
  [–*too*-rah]
  he's got a temperature ha la febbre [ah lah
  f*e*b-bray]
temporary temporaneo [–r*ah*-nay-oh]
tenere la destra *keep right*
tennis il tennis
  tennis court il campo da tennis
  tennis racket la racchetta da tennis
  [rak-k*ay*t-tah . . .]
  tennis ball la palla da tennis
tent la tenda
terminus il capolinea [ka-po-l*ee*-nay-ah]
terrible terribile [ter-r*ee*-bee-lay]
terrific magnifico [man-y*ee*-fee-koh]
than di [dee]
  bigger/older than . . . più grande/più vecchio
  di . . . [pew gr*a*n-day/pew v*e*k-yoh dee]
thanks, thank you grazie [gr*ah*-tzee-ay]
  no thank you no grazie
  thank you very much grazie tante
  [. . . t*a*n-tay]
  thank you for your help grazie per l'aiuto
  YOU MAY THEN HEAR . . .
  prego *you're welcome*
that quello

that man/that table quell'uomo/quella tavola
[kwayl-wo-moh/kwayl-lah tah-vo-lah]
I would like that one vorrei quello
[vor-ray . . .]
how do you say that? come si dice? [koh-may
see dee-chay]
the *(singular)* il, lo; la
(plural) i [ee], gli [lee]; le [lay]
theatre il teatro [tay-ah-troh]
their il loro; la loro
it's their bag/it's theirs è la loro borsa/è loro
them loro
I see them li vedo [lee vay-doh]
then allora
there lì [lee]
how do I get there? come ci arrivo? [koh-may
chee ar-ree-voh]
is there . . ./are there . . .? c'è . . ./ci sono . . .?
[cheh/chee soh-noh]
there is . . ./there are . . . c'è . . ./ci sono . . .
there you are *(giving something)* ecco
these questi
these apples queste mele [. . . may-lay]
can I take these? posso prendere questi?
[. . . pren-day-ray . . .]
they essi [es-see]
they are sono
thick spesso; *(stupid)* duro [doo-roh]
thief il ladro
thigh la coscia [koh-shah]
thin sottile [sot-tee-lay]
thing una cosa
I've lost all my things ho perso tutto quello
che avevo [o per-soh toot-toh kwayl-loh kay
a-vay-voh]
think pensare [pen-sah-ray]
I'll think it over ci penso su [chee . . . soo]
I think so/I don't think so penso di sì/di no
[pen-soh dee see . . .]

third *(adjective)* terzo [tayr-tzoh]
thirsty: I'm thirsty ho sete [o say-tay]
this questo
  this hotel/this street quest'albergo/questa strada
  can I have this one? posso avere questo?
  this is my wife/this is Mr ... questa è mia moglie/questo è il signor ... [... mee-ah mol-yay .../eel seen-yor ...]
  is this ...? è questo ... [eh ...]
those quelli; quelle [kwayl-lee kwayl-lay]
  how much are those? quanto costano? [... kos-ta-noh]
thousand mille [meel-lay]
  thousands migliaia [meel-yah-yah]
thread *(noun)* il filo [fee-loh]
three tre [tray]
throat la gola [goh-lah]
throttle l'acceleratore [a-chay-lay-ra-toh-ray]
through attraverso
  through there per di là [... dee lah]
throw *(verb)* gettare [jet-tah-ray]
thumb il pollice [pol-lee-chay]
thunder *(noun)* il tuono [twoh-noh]
  thunderstorm il temporale [−rah-lay]
Thursday giovedì [jo-vay-dee]
ticket il biglietto [beel-yet-toh]
  (cloakroom) lo scontrino [skon-tree-noh]
 » *TRAVEL TIP: see* **bus**
tie *(necktie)* la cravatta
tight *(clothes)* stretto
  they're too tight sono troppo stretti
tights il collant [ko-long]
time il tempo
  what's the time? che ore sono? [kay oh-ray ...]
  I haven't got time non ho tempo [... o ...]
  for the time being per ora
  this time/last time/next time questa volta/la

volta scorsa/la prossima [pros-see-mah] volta
3 times tre volte [tray-vol-tay]
have a good time! si diverta! [see dee-ver-tah]
timetable l'orario [o-rah-ree-oh]

» *TRAVEL TIP: how to tell the time*
it's one o'clock è l'una [eh loo-nah]
it's two/three/four o'clock sono le
due/tre/quattro [lay doo-ay/tray . . .]
it's 5/10/20/25 past seven sono le sette e
cinque/dieci/venti/venticinque [set-tay ay
cheen-kway/dee-eh-chee/vayn-tee/vayn-tee-
cheen-kway]
it's quarter past eight/eight fifteen sono le
otto e un quarto/le otto e quindici
[. . . kween-dee-chee]
it's half past nine/nine thirty sono le nove e
mezza/le nove e trenta [. . . no-vay ay
met-tzah . . .]
it's 25/20/10/5 to ten sono le dieci meno
venticinque/venti/dieci/cinque
[. . . may-noh . . .]
it's quarter to eleven/10.45 sono le undici
meno un quarto/le dieci e quarantacinque
[oon-dee-chee . . .]
it's twelve o'clock (am/pm) sono le dodici (di
mattina/di notte) [. . . doh-dee-chee . . .–tay]
at one o'clock all'una
at three thirty alle tre e trenta
tin *(can)* un barattolo [ba-rat-toh-loh]
tin-opener l'apriscatole [a-pree-skah-toh-lay]
tip *(noun)* la mancia [man-chah]
is the tip included è compresa la mancia?
[eh . . .]
» *TRAVEL TIP: same people as in UK*
tirare **pull**
tired stanco
I'm tired sono stanco
tissues i fazzolettini di carta
[ee fat-tzoh-let-tee-nee dee . . .]
to: to Rome/England a Roma/in Inghilterra

[. . . een-gheel-ter-rah]

toast il pane tostato [pah-nay tos-tah-toh]
(*drinking*) un brindisi [breen-dee-see]
» *TRAVEL TIP: 'toast' or 'tosti' in Italy are toasted*
sandwiches available as a snack in most bars

tobacco il tabacco

tobacconist's il tabaccaio [ta-bak-kah-yoh]
» *TRAVEL TIP: stamps can be bought here*

today oggi [o-jee]

toe il dito del piede [dee-toh del pee-eh-day]

together insieme [een-see-ay-may]
we're together siamo insieme
[see-ah-moh . . .]
can we pay all together? possiamo pagare
tutti insieme? [. . . pa-gah-ray . . .]

toilet la toilette [twa-let]
where are the toilets? dove sono le toilette
[doh-vay soh-noh lay twa-let]
I have to go to the toilet devo andare al
gabinetto [day-voh an-dah-ray . . .]
there's no toilet paper non c'è carta igienica
[non cheh kar-tah ee-jay-nee-kah]
» *TRAVEL TIP: see* **public convenience**

tomato un pomodoro
tomato ketchup il ketchup
tomato juice il succo di pomodoro [sook-koh
dee . . .]

tomorrow domani [dom-mah-nee]
tomorrow morning/tomorrow
afternoon/tomorrow evening
domattina/domani pomeriggio
[. . . po-may-ree-joh]/domani sera
the day after tomorrow dopodomani
see you tomorrow a domani

ton una tonnellata
» *TRAVEL TIP: 1 ton = 1,016 kilos*

tongue la lingua [leen-gwah]

tonic (water) l'acqua brillante
[. . . breel-lan-tay]

tonight stasera [stah-*say*-rah]
tonne una tonnellata
» *TRAVEL TIP: 1 tonne = 1000 kilos = metric ton*
tonsils le tonsille [ton-*seel*-lay]
tonsillitis la tonsillite [–*lee*-tay]
too troppo
  (*also*) anche [an-*kay*]
  that's too much questo è troppo [. . . eh . . .]
tool un attrezzo [at-*tret*-tzoh]
tooth un dente [*den*-tay]
  I've got toothache ho mal di denti [o . . . dee
  den-tee]
  toothbrush lo spazzolino da denti
  [spat-tzo-*lee*-noh . . .]
  toothpaste il dentifricio [den-tee-*free*-choh]
top: on top of sopra
  on the top floor all'ultimo piano
  [al-*lool*-tee-moh pee-*ah*-noh]
  at the top in cima [een *chee*-mah]
total (*noun*) il totale [toh-*tah*-lay]
tough (*meat*) duro [*doo*-roh]
tour (*noun*) un viaggio [vee-*ah*-joh]
  we'd like to go on a tour of . . . vorremmo
  visitare . . . [. . . vee-see-*tah*-ray]
  we're touring around facciamo il giro del
  paese [fa-*chah*-moh eel *jee*-roh del pah-*ay*-say]
tourist un turista
  I'm a tourist sono un turista
  tourist office l'ufficio turistico [oof-*fee*-choh
  too-*rees*-tee-koh]
tow (*verb*) rimorchiare [ree-mor-kee-*ah*-ray]
  can you give me a tow? mi può rimorchiare?
  [mee pwoh . . .]
  towrope un cavo da rimorchio [*kah*-voh dah
  ree-mor-kee-oh]
towards verso
  he was coming straight towards me veniva
  diritto verso di me [vay-*nee*-vah dee-*reet*-toh
  ver-soh dee may]

towel un asciugamano [a-shoo-ya-m*a*h-noh]
town la città [cheet-t*a*h]
  in town in città
  would you take me into the town? mi porta
  in città? [mee . . .]
traditional tradizionale
  [tra-dee-tzee-o-n*a*h-lay]
  a traditional Italian meal un pasto
  all'italiana
traffic il traffico [tr*a*f-fee-koh]
  traffic lights il semaforo [say-m*a*h-fo-roh]
  » TRAVEL TIP: *traffic lights are often suspended*
  over junctions, so watch out for this
  traffic policeman il vigile [v*ee*-jee-lay]
train il treno
  » TRAVEL TIP: *best to book in advance as trains are*
  crowded; 'rapido' is fast intercity, often
  first-class only, surcharge payable
tranquillizers i tranquillanti [–tee]
translate tradurre [tra-door-ray]
  would you translate that for me? me lo può
  tradurre? [may lo pwoh . . .]
transmission *(of car)* la trasmissione
  [tras-mees-y*oh*-nay]
travel agent's l'agenzia di viaggi [a-jen-tz*ee*-ah
  dee vee-*a*h-jee]
traveller's cheque il traveller's cheque
tree l'albero [*a*l-bay-roh]
tremendous formidabile [–d*a*h-bee-lay]
trim: just a trim please solo una spuntatina
  per favore [. . . spoon-ta-t*ee*-nah . . .]
trip *(noun)* un viaggio [vee-*a*h-joh]
  we want to go on a trip to . . . vorremmo fare
  una gita a . . . [. . . f*a*h-ray oo-nah j*ee*-tah ah]
trouble *(noun)* un disturbo [dees-t*oor*-boh]
  I'm having trouble with the steering/my
  back ho delle noie allo sterzo/dei disturbi alla
  schiena [o d*e*l-lay n*o*-yay *a*l-loh st*a*yr-tzoh/day
  dees-t*oor*-bee *a*l-lah skee-*a*y-nah]

trousers i pantaloni
true vero [vay-ro]
  it's not true non è vero [. . . eh . . .]
trunks (swimming) il costume
  [kos-too-may]
trust: I trust you ho fiducia in lei
  [o fee-doo-chah een lay]
try (verb) provare [pro-vah-ray]
  please try provi per favore [pro-vee payr
  fa-voh-ray]
  can I try it on? posso provarlo?
T-shirt una maglietta [mal-yayt-tah]
Tuesday martedì [mar-tay-dee]
turn: where do we turn off? dove voltiamo?
  [doh-vay vol-tee-ah-moh]
  he turned without indicating ha voltato
  senza indicare [ah . . . sen-tzah
  een-dee-kah-ray]
twice due volte [doo-ay vol-tay]
  twice as much il doppio [dop-pee-oh]
twin beds due letti [doo-ay let-tee]
two due [doo-ay]
typewriter la macchina da scrivere
  [mak-kee-nah dah skree-vay-ray]
typical tipico [tee-pee-koh]
tyre la gomma
  I need a new tyre ho bisogno di una nuova
  gomma [o bee-sonn-yoh dee oo-nah
  nwo-vah . . .]
» *TRAVEL TIP: tyre pressures*

lb/sq in	18	20	22	24	26	28	30
kg/sq cm	1.3	1.4	1.5	1.7	1.8	2	2.1

ugly brutto [broot-toh]
ulcer l'ulcera [ool-chay-rah]
Ulster l'Ulster [ool-ster]
umbrella l'ombrello
uncle lo zio [tzee-oh]
uncomfortable scomodo [sko-mo-doh]
unconscious inconscio [een-kon-shoh]

under sotto
underdone poco cotto
underground *(rail)* la metropolitana
understand: **I understand** capisco [ka-pee-skoh]
   I don't understand non capisco
   do you understand? capisce? [ka-pee-shay]
undo disfare [dees-fah-ray]
unfriendly scontroso
unhappy infelice [een-fay-lee-chay]
United States gli Stati Uniti [lee stah-tee oo-nee-tee]
unleaded senza piombo [sen-tzah pee-ombo]
unlock aprire [a-pree-ray]
until fino a [fee-noh ah]
   not until non prima di [. . . dee]
unusual insolito [een-so-lee-toh]
uomini gentlemen
up su [soo]
   he's not up yet non si è ancora alzato [non see eh an-koh-rah al-tzah-toh]
   what's up? cosa succede? [. . . soo-chay-day]
upside down alla rovescia [. . . ro-veh-shah]
upstairs di sopra [dee . . .]
urgent urgente [oor-jen-tay]
us: **it's not for us** non è per noi [. . .eh payr no-ee]; **can you help us?** può aiutarci? [pwoh ah-yoo-tar-chee]
uscita exit
use: **can I use . . .?** posso adoperare . . .? [rah-ray]
useful utile [oo-tee-lay]
usual solito [so-lee-toh]
   as usual come al solito [koh-may . . .]
usually di solito [dee . . .]
U-turn un'inversione [een-vers-yoh-nay]
vacancy: **do you have any vacancies?** avete una camera libera? [a-vay-tay oo-nah kah-may-rah lee-bay-rah]

vacate *(room)* lasciare vacante [la-sh*ah*-ray
va-k*a*n-tay]
vaccination la vaccinazione
[va-chee-na-tzee-*oh*-nay]
vacuum flask il thermos [t*ay*r-mos]
valanghe avalanches
valid valido [v*ah*-lee-doh]
 how long is it valid for? fino a quando è
 valido? [f*ee*-noh ah . . .]
valuable di valore [dee va-l*oh*-ray]
 my valuables i miei oggetti di valore
 [ee mee-*eh*-ee o-j*e*t-tee . . .]
value *(noun)* valore [va-l*oh*-ray]
valve la valvola [v*a*l-vo-lah]
vanilla la vaniglia [va-n*ee*l-yah]
varicose veins le vene varicose [v*a*y-nay
va-ree-k*oh*-say]
veal il vitello [vee-t*e*l-loh]
vegetables le verdure [vayr-d*oo*-ray]
vegetarian *(noun)* un vegetariano
[vay-jay-ta-ree-*ah*-noh]
ventilator il ventilatore [–t*oh*-ray] ·
vernice fresca wet paint
very molto
 very much moltissimo
via via [v*ee*-ah]
vietato fumare no smoking
village il villaggio [veel-l*ah*-joh]
vine la vite [v*ee*-tay]
vinegar l'aceto [a-ch*ay*-toh]
vineyard la vigna [v*ee*n-yah]
vintage l'annata
violent violento [vee-o-l*e*n-toh]
visibility la visibilità [–t*ah*]
visit *(verb)* visitare [vee-see-t*ah*-ray]
vodka la vodka
voice la voce [v*oh*-chay]
voltage il voltaggio [vol-t*ah*-joh]
waist la vita [v*ee*-tah]

» *TRAVEL TIP: waist measurements*

UK	24	26	28	30	32	34	36	38
Italy	61	66	71	76	80	87	91	97

wait: will we have to wait long? dobbiamo aspettare a lungo? [. . . as-payt-*tah*-ray ah loon-goh]

wait for me mi aspetti [mee . . .]

I'm waiting for a friend/my wife aspetto un amico/mia moglie [. . . oon a-m*ee*-koh/m*ee*-ah-mol-yay]

waiter il cameriere [ka-may-ree-*eh*-ray]

waiter! cameriere!

waitress la cameriera [ka-may-ree-*eh*-rah]

waitress! cameriera!

wake: will you wake me at 7.30? mi sveglia alle sette e mezza [mee sv*e*l-yah *a*l-lay s*e*t-tay ay m*e*t-tzah]

Wales il Galles [g*a*l-lays]

walk: can we walk there? possiamo andarci a piedi? [. . . an-d*a*r-chee ah pee-*eh*-dee]

are there any good walks around here? ci sono delle belle passeggiate qua? [chee s*o*h-noh d*e*l-lay b*e*l-lay pas-say-j*ah*-tay kwa]

walking shoes le scarpe da passeggio [lay sk*a*r-pay dah pas-s*a*y-joh]

walking stick il bastone da passeggio [bas-t*o*h-nay . . .]

wall il muro [m*oo*-roh]

(inside) la parete [pa-r*a*y-tay]

wallet il portafoglio [por-ta-f*o*l-yoh]

want: I want a . . . voglio un . . . [v*o*l-yoh oon]

I want to talk to . . . voglio parlare con . . . [. . . par-l*a*h-ray . . .]

what do you/does he want? che cosa vuole? [kay-ko-sah vwo-lay]

I don't want to non ne ho voglia [non nay o v*o*l-yah]

warm caldo

warning l'avviso [av-v*ee*-soh]

was: I was/he was ero/era [*eh*-roh . . .]
　it was era
wash: can you wash these for me? può
　lavarmi questi? [pwoh . . .]
　where can I wash? dove mi posso lavare?
　[d*oh*-vay mee . . . la-*vah*-ray]
　where can I wash this? dove posso lavare
　questo?
　washing machine la lavatrice
　[la-va-*tree*-chay]
　washing powder il detersivo
　[day-tayr-*see*-voh]
washer *(for nut & bolt)* la rondella
wasp la vespa
watch *(wrist-)* l'orologio [o-ro-l*oh*-joh]
　will you watch my bags for me? può
　guardarmi i bagagli? [pwoh gwar-d*ar*-mee ee
　ba-*gal*-yee]
　watch out! attento!
water l'acqua
　can I have some water? posso avere
　dell'acqua? [. . . a-v*ay*-ray . . .]
　hot and cold running water acqua corrente
　calda e fredda [. . . kor-r*en*-tay . . .]
　waterproof impermeabile
　[eem-per-may-*ah*-bee-lay]
　waterskiing lo sci nautico [shee n*ow*-
　tee-koh]
way: we'd like to eat the Italian way
　vorremmo mangiare all'italiana [. . . man-
　j*ah*-ray . . .]
　could you tell me the way to . . .? mi può
　indicare la strada per . . .? [mee pwoh
　een-dee-*kah*-ray . . .]
　see **where** *for answers*
we noi [n*o*-ee]
　we are siamo [see-*ah*-moh]
weak *(person)* debole [d*a*y-bo-lay]
weather il tempo

what filthy weather! che tempo schifoso! [kay tem-poh skee-foh-soh]

what's the weather forecast? quali sono le previsioni del tempo? [kwah-lee soh-noh lay pray-vee-see-oh-nee . . .]

YOU MAY THEN HEAR . . .

pioverà [pee-o-vay-rah] *it is going to rain*

farà bel tempo [fa-rah . . .] *it's going to be fine*

Wednesday mercoledì [mer-ko-lay-dee]

week la settimana

a week today oggi a otto [o-jee . . .]

at the weekend al weekend

weight il peso

well: I'm not feeling well non mi sento bene [non mee sen-toh bay-nay]

he's not well non sta bene

how are you? – very well, thanks come sta? – bene, grazie [koh-may stah – bay-nay grah-tzee-ay]

you speak English very well parla un buon inglese [. . . bwon een-glay-say]

wellingtons gli stivali di gomma [lee stee-vah-lee dee . . .]

Welsh gallese [gal-lay-say]

were: you were era [eh-rah]

(*familiar*) eri

(*plural*) eravate [eh-ra-vah-tay]

we were eravamo

they were erano [eh-ra-noh]

west ovest [o-vest]

West Indies le Indie Occidentali [een-dee-ay o-chee-dayn-tah-lee]

wet bagnato [ban-yah-toh]

(*weather*) umido [oo-mee-doh]

wet suit la tuta da sub [too-tah dah soob]

what cosa

what is that? cos'è questo? [koh-seh . . .]

what for? perché [payr-kay]

wheel la ruota [rwo-tah]

when quando
   when is breakfast? a che ora è la colazione?
   [ah kay *oh*-rah eh lah ko-la-tzee-*oh*-nay]
where dove [d*oh*-vay]
   where is the post office? dov'è l'ufficio
   postale? [doh-v*eh* loof-*fee*-choh pos-t*ah*-lay]
YOU MAY THEN HEAR ...
diritto *straight on*
a destra *to the right*
a sinistra *to the left*
torni in dietro *go back*
which quale [kw*ah*-lay]
   which one? quale
YOU MAY THEN HEAR ...
questo *this one* quello *that one*
whisky il whisky
white bianco [bee-*a*n-koh]
Whitsun la Pentecoste [–tay]
who chi [kee]
wholesale all'ingrosso
whose di chi [dee kee]
   whose is this? di chi è questo?
YOU MAY THEN HEAR ...
è mio *it's mine*
è suo *it's his/it's hers*
why perché [payr-k*ay*]
   why not? perché no?
wide largo
wife: my wife mia moglie [m*ee*-ah m*o*l-yay]
will: when will it be finished? quando sarà
   pronto?
   will you do it? lo fa lei? [. . . lay]
   I will come back tomorrow torno domani
wind *(noun)* il vento
window la finestra [fee-n*e*s-trah]
   near the window vicino alla finestra
   [vee-ch*ee*-noh . . .]
windscreen il parabrezza [pa-ra-br*ay*t-tzah]
   windscreen wipers i tergicristalli [ee

tayr-jee-krees-tal-lee]

windy: it is windy today oggi c'è vento [o-jee cheh ven-toh]

wine il vino [vee-noh]

can I see the wine list? posso avere la lista dei vini? [. . . a-vay-ray lah lees-tah day vee-nee]

» *TRAVEL TIP: best wines show D.O.C. (Denominazione d'Origine Controllata) and the place where bottled (cantine di . . .) on the label;*

Barolo, Barbera, Barbaresco *full-bodied reds from Piedmont, go well with roasts and venison;*

Bardolino, Valpolicella *light reds, go well with all kinds of meat;*

Pinot Bianco/Grigio *dry whites from Friuli;*

Lambrusco *sparkling red from Emilia;*

Frascati *white, dry or sweet, from near Rome;*

Chianti *red and white, from Tuscany, (the best is Chianti Classico);*

Verdicchio *dry white from Marche, very good with fish;*

Vernaccia *dry white from Sardinia, very strong and aromatic*

winter l'inverno

wire il filo metallico [fee-loh may-tal-lee-koh] *(electrical)* il filo eletrico

wish: best wishes tanti auguri

with con

without senza [sen-tzah]

witness testimone [tes-tee-moh-nay]

will you act as a witness for me? mi può fare da testimone? [mee pwoh fah-ray . . .]

woman la donna

women le donne [don-nay]

wonderful meraviglioso [may-ra-veel-yoh-soh]

won't: it won't start non parte [–tay]

wood *(trees)* il bosco

it's made of wood è di legno [eh di layn-yoh]

wool la lana

word la parola

I don't know that word non conosco quella parola

work *(verb)* lavorare [la-vo-*rah*-ray]
 it's not working non funziona [. . . foon-tzee-*oh*-nah]
 I work in London lavoro a Londra

worry: I'm worried about him sono preoccupato per lui [. . . *loo*-ee]
 don't worry non si preoccupi

worse: it's worse è peggio [eh *peh*-joh]
 he's getting worse sta peggiorando [stah pay-jo-*ra*n-doh]

worst il peggio [*peh*-joh]

worth: it's not worth that much non vale tanto [. . . v*ah*-lay . . .]
 is it worthwhile going to . . .? vale la pena di andare a . . .? [v*ah*-lay lah p*a*y-nah dee an-d*ah*-ray ah]

wrap: could you wrap it up? mi può fare un pacchetto? [mee pwoh f*ah*-ray oon pak-k*a*yt-toh]

wrench *(noun: tool)* la chiave inglese [kee-*ah*-vay een-gl*a*y-say]

wrist il polso

write scrivere [skr*ee*-vay-ray]
 could you write it down? può scriverlo? [pwoh . . .]
 I'll write to you ti scrivo [tee skr*ee*-voh]
 writing paper la carta da lettere [. . . l*e*t-tay-ray]

wrong sbagliato [sbal-y*ah*-toh]
 I think the bill's wrong penso che il conto sia sbagliato
 there's something wrong with . . . c'è qualcosa che non va con . . . [cheh kwal-*ko*-sa kay . . .]
 you're wrong lei ha torto [lay ah t*or*-toh]
 sorry, wrong number scusi, ho sbagliato numero [sk*oo*-zee, o sbal-y*ah*-toh n*oo*-may-roh]

....

X-ray una radiografia [ra-dee-o-gra-*fee*-ah]
yacht lo yacht
yard *(measurement)* una iarda [y*a*r-dah]
» *TRAVEL TIP: 1 yard = 91.44 cm = 0.91 m*
year l'anno
   this year/next year quest'anno/l'anno
   prossimo [. . . pr*o*s-see-moh]
yellow giallo [j*a*l-loh]
yes sì [see]
yesterday ieri [y*e*h-ree]
   the day before yesterday l'altroieri
   [al-tro-y*e*h-ree]
   yesterday morning/afternoon ieri
   mattina/ieri pomeriggio [. . . po-may-ree-joh]
yet: is it ready yet? è già pronto? [eh djah . . .]
   not yet non ancora
yoghurt lo yoghurt
you lei [lay]
   (familiar) tu [too]
   (plural) voi [v*o*-ee]
   I can't hear you non la/ti/vi sento [. . . tee
   vee . . .]
   I'll send it to you glielo spedisco
   [lee-*a*y-loh . . .]/te lo spedisco [tay . . .]/ve lo
   spedisco [vay . . .]
   with you con lei/te/voi
   is that you? è lei/sei tu/siete voi? [eh lay/say
   too/see-*a*y-tay vo-ee]
» *TRAVEL TIP: only use the 'tu' form with good
friends*
young giovane [j*o*h-va-nay]
your suo [s*oo*-oh]; tuo [t*oo*-oh]; vostro
   see **you**
   is this your camera, is this yours? è questa
   la sua/tua macchina fotografica, è sua/tua
   questa? [eh . . . m*a*k-kee-nah
   photo-gr*a*h-fee-kah . . .]
youth hostel l'ostello per la gioventù
   [. . . jo-ven-*too*]

Yugoslavia la Jugoslavia [yoo-go . . .]
Yugoslavian jugoslavo
zero zero [tz*eh*-roh]
   below zero sotto zero
zip la cerniera [chayr-nee-*eh*-rah]
zona disco *parking disc zone*

The Italian Alphabet
*letters in brackets don't actually exist in the Italian
alphabet but are useful for spelling English names
etc*

a [ah]
b [bee]
c [chee]
d [dee]
e [ay]
f [effay]
g [gee]
h [akka]
i [ee]
(j) [ee lunga]
(k) [kappa]
l [ellay]
m [emmay]
n [ennay]
o [oh]
p [pee]
q [koo]
r [erray]
s [essay]
t [tee]
u [oo]
v [voo]
(w) [voo doppio]
(x) [eeks]
(y) [ee-greka]
z [tzay-tah]

Numbers

0 zero [tzay-roh]

1 uno [*oo*-noh]	6 sei [say]
2 due [d*oo*-ay]	7 sette [s*et*-tay]
3 tre [tray]	8 otto
4 quattro	9 nove [n*o*-vay]
5 cinque [ch*ee*n-kway]	10 dieci [dee-*eh*-chee]

11 undici [*oo*n-dee-chee]
12 dodici [d*oh*-dee-chee]
13 tredici [tr*a*y-dee-chee]
14 quattordici [kwat-t*o*r-dee-chee]
15 quindici [kw*ee*n-dee-chee]
16 sedici [s*a*y-dee-chee]
17 diciassette [dee-chas-s*et*-tay]
18 diciotto [dee-ch*o*t-toh]
19 diciannove [dee-chan-n*o*-vay]

20 venti	21 ventuno
22 ventidue	23 ventitré
24 ventiquattro	25 venticinque
26 ventisei	27 ventisette
28 ventotto	29 ventinove

30 trenta	31 trentuno
40 quaranta	50 cinquanta
60 sessanta	70 settanta
80 ottanta	90 novanta

100 cento [ch*e*n-toh]
101 centouno [chen-toh-*oo*-noh]
165 centosessantacinque
200 duecento
1000 mille [m*ee*l-lay]
2000 duemila [doo-ay-m*ee*-lah]